"*Boomerang*, the modern day evidence of a Father's arms—wide open—waiting and calling for us—the new generation of prodigals—to embrace His love, believe His truth, and to be transformed by His grace. Are any of us beyond hope? *Boomerang* says, 'No!' And that's the power found in this hope!"

—Kevin McCullough
Nationally Syndicated Television/Radio Host

"Brett Rickey is a leading voice in the church today. His insight and humor make the truths of scripture come to life. I've known Brett for over a decade, and he lives what he writes. Free from 'Christian fluff and jargon' his books offer practical insight and application to everyday life."

—Brad Farnsworth
Lead Pastor
Connection Church

"There are many things I could say about Brett Rickey, but the first one that comes to mind is he is the real deal. As a follower of Christ, husband, father, leader, and writer, authenticity is all over him, with the added benefit of humor. What Brett shares in these pages will not only cause you to look at God in a whole new way, you may also discover a surprising new work taking place in you."

—Dan Huckins
Lead Pastor
Lima Community Church

BOOMERANG

BOOMERANG

THE RETURN OF THE PRODIGAL SON

BRETT RICKEY

BEACON HILL PRESS
OF KANSAS CITY

Library of Congress Cataloging-in-Publication Data
Rickey, Brett, 1963-
  Boomerang : the return of the prodigal son / Brett Rickey.
    p. cm.
  Includes bibliographical references (p.).
  ISBN 978-0-8341-2735-7 (pbk.)
  1. Prodigal son (Parable) I. Title.
  BT378.P8R54 2011
  226.4'06--dc23
                                   2011022588

10 9 8 7 6 5 4 3 2

CONTENTS

INTRODUCTION

I made very few purchases on my own during my teenage years since I had not yet become financially independent. My income sources early on consisted mostly of warm-weather employment when I was paid to wash Mom's car, cut the grass, or pull weeds at our church. But during those years I was able to buy a couple things that I'm proud of today—very manly items that still make me smile as I wonder what I ever did with them anyway.

The two items were a "Wrist-Rocket" slingshot and the authentic Wham-O red plastic boomerang. Both of these pieces of pseudo-weaponry oozed danger, intrigue, and possible physical harm—in other words, candy to a teenager.

The "Wrist-Rocket" was cool to look at and fun to use but difficult to aim. I tried like crazy to master the instructions and aim just the way the picture showed, but no luck. I could hit a ninety-gallon drum from twenty yards but soon concluded that slingshot accuracy like that won't feed a guy lost in the wilderness for long. Bears don't usually go down from small rocks pummeled to the abdomen. The slingshot didn't hold my attention very long.

The boomerang was a different kind of thing, though. I understood that the purpose of the returning boomerang was more elegant than dangerous. Throwing it correctly was just plain fun. The idea for the returning boomerang, I have since learned, was not to be used as a weapon, though it could inflict bodily harm if it hit a man on the noggin. The returning boomerang is simply used as a cool sporting device that can fly from the hand of the thrower, travel a specific distance, and then return to the place from which it was thrown. There is a trick to it—to throw it well takes practice.

The instructions that accompanied my new purchase contained a diagram of the way my right arm should angle at the point of release. The picture showed that I should bend my arm at the elbow a precise forty-five degrees from the ground before I let it fly. I tried it their way, but I was clearly doing something wrong. I would throw it, but it would fly and land a long way from me. I tried it over and over, but my first day of boomerang throwing was a failure.

I didn't give up, though. I used a big mirror in the house to help me. I compared my arm angle in the mirror to the one on the diagram and was able to correct and diagnose part of my problem.

I went back outside with this new information and got closer to making the boomerang return to me, but something was still a little off. I went back to the diagram and analyzed it again. Bingo! I saw something new. To this point, I had mastered the arm angle of the throw, but I hadn't understood the principle of the release point. I was basically aiming my throw up toward the clouds and releasing it that way. The in-structions showed that I should release the boomerang with a downward trajectory, which made it nearly hit the ground before sailing up and back. The key element I was missing was in the release. After a little practice, it wasn't that hard, and the returning boomerang actually returned.

One day recently as I was thinking back on that time in my life, God spoke to me through memories and images and my own inner voice. I got to thinking about the idea of release and love. I'm currently going through my first big round of parental release as my oldest has gone off to college this year. It was a difficult transition that I'm still not fully okay with. Releasing your baby to the world is never an easy thing to do.

But I also know that my children were never mine to begin with, and part of the fun of raising children is to watch them grow up and do what God created them to do. An oft-quoted adage says, "If you love someone, you will set them free," and I know there is some truth in that. But it's easier to say than do.

Jesus once told a story about a father that seemed to be very comfortable with the idea of release. In this story, the father releases his wild and wayward son from his responsibilities at home and sends him out with a wad of money—thanks to an early tapping of the son's inheritance. The father is obviously well aware of his son's lack of character and moral fiber, yet he releases him anyway. He releases him with generosity and grace.

It seems a little enabling and weak-minded initially, but in the end we see the one who was released coming back to the very place he was released from to the very person who released him. There was something in that initial release that made a safe return home possible; and there was something implanted in that son—by his father—that made coming back home an attractive alternative to life in the pigsty the son ultimately encountered while he was away.

This story is widely known as the story of the prodigal son, found in the Bible in the Book of Luke, chapter 15. It's a story about the boomerang-like path of a crazy son, his loving father, and his dependable older brother. I have heard this story since childhood, and each time I have read it as an adult, I've glazed over it because of its hyper-familiarity. Sometimes it's easy to overlook the best things in life because they've been seen so often.

But there came a day when this story became very real to me as I saw it for the first time through someone else's eyes. Here's how it went down.

ONE
THE SHOWDOWN AT STARBUCKS

I was right in the middle of one of those rare, unplanned you-just-had-to-be-there-to-believe-it moments at my favorite place away from home—Starbucks. Starbucks purposefully creates this affable, living room-type atmosphere in their stores. Their corporate mission actually involves creating a "third place," after home and work, where a person can relax, make friends, and just hang out. Starbucks' evil plan has worked so well in my case that I make it my second office when working on the talks I give to my home church each week. Much of this book was done there as well.

So I was hanging out, enjoying my vacation near Bradenton, Florida, reading and journaling and having my alone time with God. I like to be alone in my alone time, and I don't like rude people who laugh too much on their cell phones inside my pristine coffee castle. Starbucks should feel more like a cool library than a train station, but some people are clueless and lack any kind of basic self-awareness and should have been trained better at home but weren't. These same "some people" still have a problem understanding cellular technology and sound amplification and feel the need to raise their voices to be heard, even when talking about personal issues, which can be a little embarrassing and annoying at the same time. I have real issues with loud talkers who invade my ear space inside Starbucks. That's all I'm saying. And if you're one of them, you have no idea what I'm talking about.

Okay, I was about halfway done with my venti vanilla coffee when this all went down. And after you read this, you may feel that I have taken liberties to make the story more interesting or colorful. Let me assure you—this is really what happened.

Feeling devoted and close to God in the moment, I was writing my prayer in my journal when this sixty-ish gentleman walked in and sat down and began speaking to this twenty-something guy at the corner table. I noticed the contrast in the way they were groomed. The older guy was obviously a local—dark tan to go with his white crew-cut. His affect was bulldog tough—very militaristic and confident.

The younger man, on the other hand, seemed to be the kind of person you would see hanging out at Starbucks in the mother-ship store on Pike Place in Seattle—very relaxed, with wavy hair and glasses. He gave off a kind of beatnik-European attitude. He probably liked Emily Dickinson and Robert Frost—that kind of look.

I assume from the way the older man entered and spoke that he had an appointment or was expected by the younger. But that's when things got strange and my assumptions were altered. The older man sat down and began what I can only describe to you as some kind of pseudo-Christian, I-want-to-help-you-on-my-own-terms tirade. He began by saying rather loudly, "Do you have any money or means of support?" He didn't wait for an answer and stated, "Fifteen years ago I was right where you are. No money, no house, no job, but now I'm out of that. My wife and I are Christian people, and I have some money. We want to help people like you. But you need to take some kind of initiative in this deal."

The young man—I later learned his name is Jason—responded by saying, "Sir, I don't have much money, and I don't have a place to stay right now."

Again, without listening, the older man said, "Here's the deal. I will take you right now to Salvation Army. You can stay there for three days and eat for free, and they can help you get on your feet. That's my final offer, and you can either accept it or reject it. It's up to you. Do what you want to do, but I won't offer it again!"

Jason asked, "Uh, can I get your name and phone number?"

The man responded by saying abruptly, "No, I will not give you my number, but my first name is Bill, that's all you're getting!"

Jason said that he didn't need a place to stay, and as he was trying to explain why, the older man interrupted again, saying, "Your problem is that you don't want to take responsibility for your life. You just want to sit here drinking coffee"—to which the Jason replied, "Okay, now you're judging me, and you don't even know me."

The older man became very agitated and replied, "Well, that was my final offer. I've done my Christian thing, so now I'm leaving!"

Jason replied kindly, "So this was just about appeasing your conscience? I don't need your help, but I thank you for the offer." And the older man walked out the door.

All of this took about three minutes—a lot of talking and a lot of listening, and the Christian wasn't listening. I was sick. Jason returned quietly to his book. Starbucks was silent, no steaming or chit-chat as the room had emptied. The only thing hanging in the air was the strong aroma of coffee originating from the mountains of Ethiopia.

I'm on vacation. Back home I'm a pastor; but in Bradenton, Florida, I'm a nobody with a tourist T-shirt and peeling skin from being overcooked on the beach. I have purposefully taken a longer-than-usual vacation to renew and relax as this particular year had been very stressful on me personally. I'm not at Starbucks to be a pastor, as if I had any choice in the deal. But this was something I couldn't overlook. I had just witnessed some kind of Christian drive-by shooting in which someone, speaking in the name of Jesus, had done everything absolutely wrong. By his attitude he blasphemed the very heart of our merciful Lord Jesus and killed the Lord's witness to anyone else inside the store at that moment. This was a conversation that everyone heard, and one that made the Christian look like the bad guy—which he was—and made Jason look like the victim—which he was. This was religion at its worst; the kind of religion keeping people away from Jesus by the millions in the United States. It's the same kind of religion that made Jesus sick in His day too.

It took me a couple of minutes of wrestling with God to muster the confidence to finally say something. By nature, I'm more introverted. I like to watch and think and write and learn and, when called upon, to express my ideas after I have adequate preparation. I don't need a lot of social interaction to be happy. I find energy from being alone. I also know that the Bible says that in my weakness God is strong if I submit and let Him do the working.

My first words across the quiet coffee shop to Jason were, "Uh, I couldn't help but notice . . . what happened?"

He said, "Do you mind if I come over to your table?"

"Sure—come on over," I said.

I repeated that I had heard the gist of the conversation, and he said, "Yeah, the place cleared out pretty quickly, didn't it?"

This was a fact that I had somehow missed in the moment. "So what's up? What was that all about?"

Jason said the story was long, and I replied that I had plenty of time, which is the good part of being on vacation. I had decided up front that I could at least listen and maybe somehow attempt to rebuild a kind of bridge that the zealous "Christianator" had just blown away.

I found out a lot about Jason. He had just come back to the United States from Europe, where he had a first child on the way. He came home to stay with his father with the idea that he could perhaps find a job to support his new family and move them to the United States soon. The job search had not gone well, and neither had his reconnection with his family in the United States. He was staying with his grandmother, who had just asked him to leave.

I was a little wary on this point and still not sure I got the whole story, but he said their family disagreement stemmed from the fact that he felt the need to point out their duplicity in life—how they said one thing yet did another. I know that was his view, and I didn't know the other side; only God knows why he got kicked out of Grandma's house. But at that moment the "why" didn't really matter.

He went on to say that his dad had promised to take him to another town to look for work. Early that morning Jason had put a note on his dad's car explaining that he was ready to go and welcomed a ride. He had spent the previous night on a bench outside a Wal-Mart and now at 10 A.M. was here waiting on his dad, who was obviously avoiding him.

All this made me even more curious about the origins of Mr. White Crew Cut. I said, "So who was that guy?" I still believed that he had to be a relative.

Jason replied that he didn't even know the guy. He was apparently a neighbor of the grandmother who took it upon himself to attempt to save the day—in the name of Jesus, of course. He walked into Jason's life and offered something right out of a Marvel comic strip: the hideous creature with a big mouth, little hands, and tiny ears, wearing a cross and a crew cut.

After twenty minutes of talking, Jason asked the big question—the question that sometimes ends conversations. He said, "So what do you do?"

I hesitated, took a deep breath, and replied timidly, "I'm a pastor on vacation," after which I quickly asked him his plans and hopes and about his life in Europe—anything to get the focus off me and my title.

He spoke very eloquently for a while, and as he talked, I got the impression from God that I needed to help him see the Father's possible involvement in the events of this day.

I said, "You know, I was just reading the Bible this morning, and there was once this guy named Hezekiah. The Bible says that he was a very righteous guy and that he tried to do his best and that because of this, God really blessed him." I did my best to explain how God wanted to bless him, Jason, as well. I hoped he would understand that God is a good God who has good plans for His kids.

To my surprise, he appeared interested in what I had to say. I can usually tell when people are tuning me out, but he wasn't. So I pressed on.

"You know about Jesus, right?" And he nodded. "Jesus had a favorite story about two brothers and a dad. The younger one said 'Dad, I don't want to wait until you die—I want my inheritance now.'"

Jason's eyes expressed shock, and he said, "No way!" This was a new story to him, and he was getting into it.

"So the young son took his money and partied hard and spent it all and was pretty-much homeless. He ended up working in a pig farm feeding pigs, which for a Jewish boy would be the worst job ever. He was so hungry he even wanted to eat what he was feeding the pigs! Remember: Jesus was a Jew talking to Jews. So then the young son had an idea to go back home. He reasoned that he could ask for forgiveness, work for his dad, and at least would have some food to eat and a roof over his head." Jason was still listening, so I continued.

"Okay, so when he heads home, before he even gets there, the father who had given him all the money sees him coming home and runs to meet him—meaning that he had been looking for him to come home for a while now. The younger son confesses his mistake and asks for a job, but the dad says, 'Hey, forget that! It's party time here at the ranch. You were lost, but now you're home. I'm so happy you're home!' The Father didn't do guilt trips. No condemnation, just joy that the son had come home."

I said, "Jason, the father in the story is all about God our Father. He has a great plan for your life now, and what you've done in the past is over. He just wants to hang out with you and be your guide in life, and if you follow Him, He'll bless everything you do."

I said, "Now there was an older brother in the story. He complained about the father's mercy. He thought he'd kept all the rules and that this was what being a good son was about. But the father corrected him and said, 'Son, you've totally missed the point of being my son! Come on in and eat a big family meal, on me!' But the older brother wouldn't eat with the younger, and he missed out on the party of the decade. He thought he was better than all of that. He had kept the rules, and that was all that needed to be done."

Then I slowed down and said, "Jason, the guy who was here earlier was a lot like that older brother. He missed the point of being God's son. He was mad and mean-spirited, and I'm sorry that you had to deal with him."

I was stunned by the look on his face. He had something that he didn't have earlier. It looked a lot like hope. I was stunned also by the impact of this simple story. I had told it to congregations and small groups before but had never told it to a person one-on-one who was hearing it for the very first time. But after telling it to Jason, I wanted to find other guys like him to tell it to. It was a life-changing day for both of us.

At this point I didn't lead him in the sinner's prayer. Some would say that I failed to close the deal and missed my opportunity. I understand their critique, but I didn't see it that way. I just said to him what I would want someone to say to me in a similar situation. I said, "Jason, I'll be praying for you today. I know the Creator of the universe loves you, and He will reveal himself to you today. So when He does, I want to encourage you to talk with Him and ask Him for His help."

He said he would. We talked more about his view of spiritual things, and I probed a little into his New-Age-Eastern-mystic-I'm-still-searching background, but the seed that God had wanted to plant got planted. I gave him my card and encouraged him to e-mail me about his journey and told him I would be in touch as well. I still don't know what will come of Jason or what value our conversation will have in spurring any kind of change in his life. Change is always difficult.

All I do know is that when I was telling the story of the prodigal son to Jason, I saw the freshness and wonder in Jason's eyes that Jesus probably saw when He first told it. And as I told it, something inside me changed again. I can't get enough of that story. It's the kind of story a person can write a book about. And after feeling God's prompting and viewing what I viewed at Starbucks, I was sure that God wanted a reminder sent out to all who will read this.

This book will be broken into three different movements relating to the three characters in the story of the prodigal son: the youngest son, the oldest son, and the father. I know in these three characters you will find yourself in some of the scenes happening in life right now.

If you're like me, your current life story is something similar to reading the comics page in the morning newspaper. You have a lot of boxes representing a lot of problems and relationships and conversations and stories in various forms of completion. Most of the assorted chronicles aren't related, except that you're a part of all the boxes. You are in every scene, like it or not. On the front left-hand corner you probably have the funny stuff, like "Garfield" or "Marmaduke." These are the bits and pieces of life that are bringing you some measure of joy and serve as a great escape from the rest. But you also most certainly have some ongoing drama with a new twist today. I remember reading the pug-nosed policeman comic "Dick Tracy," and my mom used to read the serial "Prince Valiant." There was always a lot of drama happening with Dick and the good prince, as is the case with most of us most of the time. (I live with a wife, three kids, and a female dog. My life has much drama.)

And then there's always the superhero section of your life. These are the scenes that are putting a knot in your stomach right now. You really do need a superhero to fix it and end the angst. And like the comics section, our lives are slowly paced where change moments happen over long periods of time.

I really believe the prodigal son was Jesus' favorite story. It's a story that can be part of the change process in all the different scenes you face today. My hunch and my hope is that you will find yourself relating to all three characters in some new ways during the course of your reading. I know I can learn much from the loving father, the grumpy son, and his wild and crazy brother. I'm sure that somewhere, with someone, right now, I share those same relational tendencies.

So whether you have followed Jesus since you were a child or you don't like the Christian message and are still searching for more answers in life—even if you may lean toward being the older brother in your story—God the Father's response to everyone is simple: Welcome home.

Can You Relate?

Read through the following questions and record your thoughts and reactions.

1. Do you think the term "pseudo Christian" is being a little tough on the man who approached Jason at Starbucks? Or do you think calling him a Christian is being a little too easy on him? Do you think he accomplished what he purportedly set out to accomplish? Explain. Can you defend his words and behavior? Explain.

_____

_____

_____

_____

_____

_____

_____

_____

_____

_____

_____

_____

_____

2. Name some of the obvious and maybe not-so-obvious reasons Jason declined his offer. Describe Jason's feelings and thoughts.

_____

_____

_____

_____

_____

_____

_____

_____

_____

_____

_____

_____

_____

_____

_____

_____

_____

_____

_____

3. Have you ever been on either end of a "Christian drive-by shooting"? Can you think of ways either of the participants in the conversation could have helped steer the exchange to a better end? Do you think Bill felt satisfied by the conversation? Why or why not? How about Jason?

_____

_____

_____

_____

_____

_____

_____

_____

_____

_____

_____

_____

_____

_____

_____

_____

4. There's a television show called "What Would You Do?" that is popular right now. Let's play the Christian version. If you had witnessed this showdown at Starbucks, what do you think you would have done? Would you have engaged Jason in conversation? Would you have interrupted Bill's tirade? Would you have spoken with Jason after Bill left and shown him what Christian compassion really is? Describe how you would have handled the same or a similar situation.

_____

_____

_____

_____

_____

_____

_____

_____

_____

_____

_____

_____

_____

_____

_____

5. In the days following the Starbucks incident, which message do you think Jason spent the most time thinking about—Bill's or Brett's? Why?

_____

_____

_____

_____

_____

_____

_____

_____

_____

_____

_____

_____

_____

_____

_____

_____

_____

6. Which of the three main characters in the showdown at Starbucks do you relate to most—the loving father, the grumpy son, the wild and wandering son? Do you see something of each in yourself? In what ways?

_____

_____

_____

_____

_____

_____

_____

_____

_____

_____

_____

_____

_____

_____

_____

_____

_____

SECTION ONE

Lost Outside
(Young Son)

TWO
WHAT HAPPENS IN VEGAS . . .

The younger son got together all he had, set off for a distant country and there squandered his wealth in wild living.

—Luke 15:13

I've never been to "The Strip" and have only had a brief layover at the airport there. But like you, I know the motto of the city that rarely sleeps.

Las Vegas has never had any real appeal to me. I'm not that interested in Wayne Newton or watching any of the scores of entertainers who are past their prime and charge premium prices to sing songs that always sound better on the CD anyway. I also don't gamble and figure that I don't need to add that temptation to my life. Mindy and I just don't see the need to make it there, even though the thought still crosses my mind that it would be really fascinating to see all the architecture and the buildings designed as human conveyor belts to depravity and greed.

About fourteen or so years ago, I noticed a concerted campaign proclaiming that Las Vegas was changing its image. One of my work friends clued me in that apparently some of the city fathers decided they would make more money if they became a family-friendly place and marketed to regular people—families with two and a half kids—not just deranged hedonists. I remember seeing the shiny magazine and television ads proclaiming this newer, cleaner image that would keep the sinning part out of the view of tender eyes. Las Vegas was committed to trying harder to prove its critics wrong. Obviously, looking back and from a distance, it seems they were trying to change the outside of the package, but the package was still the same. In a short time, this new marketing idea was scrapped for some old-fashioned, honest self-indulgence. Sin sells well, it seems.

Shortly after that, the slogan that many of us know came to be: "What happens in Vegas stays in Vegas." I'm not sure who wrote it down first, but this slogan is one of the catchiest lies conceived in the hearts of humanity. It just rolls off the tongue and makes good people feel a little naughty for even saying it. But what it hides is so dangerous to the human soul because it provides people with the false belief that life can be compartmentalized by geography— that somehow I can be bad out West and still be a good person. As a pastor, I can tell you for certain there is no geographical consequence-free zone.

If you go to Vegas and dig a big hole of debt, it will follow you home. If you catch a sexually transmitted disease in Vegas, the doctor back home will be dealing with it. If you go to Vegas and violate your marriage vows, your spouse won't just let it go because it didn't happen close to home. Sin is not a matter of geography, and it can't be compartmentalized. Sin may be fun for a season, but the negative consequences can last for millennia by comparison. The truth is "What happens in Vegas—or any other place like it—always stays with you." That is probably not going to be the slogan Vegas trots out next year.

Jesus tells us that the prodigal ventured to a distant country, the idea being that he was getting as far away from the father as possible. He wanted to sow some wild oats for sure, as kids still do on spring break every year at Cancún and Daytona. But what he didn't consider was the fact that what happens in a "distant country" never really stays there either. He was deceived into believing that the god of pleasure would bring eternal fun for all. As he soon found out, money runs out and sin always has a payday and costs a person more than he or she ever imagined.

One of the things I like to do for my personal devotional reading is read through the One-Year Bible. It is laid out with a reading from the Old Testament, New Testament, Psalms, and Proverbs every day. The best thing about the one-year Bible is that it forces you to read things you would usually choose to skip. The Book of Numbers is one of those books I probably wouldn't read without this discipline, because it has a lot of numbers and names of people that don't mean a lot to me. Numbers also has a lot of stories that open the heart of God to me, because it is all about God's people on a journey and how He deals with them along the way.

This particular traveling group was the nation of Israel on the way from Egypt to the Promised Land. However, there are parallels all over the place of how God deals with His children today on their individual journeys.

I have to admit that some of the stories at first glance seem to portray God as harsh. I'm confused sometimes by trying to reconcile the character of God in Numbers with the person of Jesus Christ I find in the Gospels. I'm beginning to understand that sometimes the best thing for me to do is not to try to figure God out but to try to hear what He was saying back then to people He loved very much and hear what new thing He is saying to me through that. With that thought, at first glance this story makes me scratch my head.

Let me give you some background first.

Israel is traveling toward the Promised Land, and God is blessing them. They have already defeated the Amorites and are gaining a reputation as a fearsome foe. They now settle down as a large group on the edge of an area known as Moab. The leader of the Moabites is a character named Balak, who is alarmed and at a loss as to what he should do to these people in his neighborhood. So he hatches a plan to invite the famous prophet Balaam to town and asks him to curse the Israelites for a large sum of money.

Balaam, a sketchy character with apparent spiritual abilities, agrees but states he will speak only what God tells him to speak. He can't prophesy doom unless God tells him to. So Balaam asks God to give him the words to say, and on four separate occasions Balaam utters words of blessing about Israel's future—because that is what God tells him to say. Balak is very angry at the lack of cursing, and they go their separate ways. This all happens in Numbers 22 through 24.

So after I read those chapters, I remembered that I had heard the name "Balaam" used in a negative way too. In these passages he seems to be a questionable fellow, but apparently God speaks through him, and he doesn't do anything bad that I could read. So I did a search of his name in the Bible and found this in the last book of the Bible:

> To the angel of the church in Pergamum write: Nevertheless, I have a few things against you: You have

people there who hold to the teaching of Balaam, who taught Balak to entice the Israelites to sin by eating food sacrificed to idols and by committing sexual immorality. *(Revelation 2:12, 14)*

Apparently Balaam didn't curse Israel from the outside, but he was able to let Balak in on a little secret. The little secret is that you get far more flies with honey than you do with vinegar. In other words, if you want to beat a foe who's stronger on the outside, you have to find a way to weaken him or her on the inside first.

The little secret is the same one I used in our home to kill an ant problem a few years back. Wherever I saw the ant trails, the instructions told, I was to put an attractant out that had a combination of sugar and boric acid. Going down, the sugar tastes good to the ant apparently; but the boric acid is a deadly chaser. Within days whole ant colonies are destroyed from the inside out.

Look at how Israel responds to the sugar in Numbers 25 that Balaam taught Balak to use.

While Israel was staying in Shittim, the men began to indulge in sexual immorality with Moabite women who invited them to the sacrifices to their gods. The people ate and bowed down before these gods. So Israel joined in worshiping the Baal of Peor. And the LORD's anger burned against them. *(Numbers 25:1-3)*

Verse 2 shows us that this was not an accidental slip-up; this was an invitation by the enemy. It was a coordinated attack that went right after the heart of the men and did a lot more damage than anticipated. So why do you think these guys were such easy marks?

Well, from a modern standpoint, let's empathize a minute with these poor wandering Israelites and give them a hip-sounding justification for their activities.

First, they lived in tents. What kind of life is that? And to top it off, they were drifting around the desert and probably bored silly at times. Since the miracle of television hadn't been invented yet, there wasn't much to do. So who could blame the boys for blowing off a little steam with the locals? I mean, every young man has a God-given right to sow his wild oats in whatever field he finds himself, right? And if that means a moral slip-up now and again, who's counting? They reasoned sex is fun, God created sex and fun, so then He must want us to have fun and therefore must want us to have sex frequently—as an act of worship, of course. These sly women may have even used the line "What happens in Moab stays in Moab!"—in another language, I mean.

What may have been perceived as a little slip-up was a mighty big deal to God. This is one of those passages that shows me a side of God that I would rather not see, especially when I'm not listening the way I should.

> The LORD said to Moses, "Take all the leaders of these people, kill them and expose them in broad daylight before the LORD, so that the LORD's fierce anger may turn away from Israel." So Moses said to Israel's judges, "Each of you must put to death those of your

men who have joined in worshiping the Baal of Peor."
(Numbers 25:4-5)

Apparently for God, the sin was so egregious and widespread that swift and deadly action had to take place. Initially, the campaign to get the sin didn't work very well. So the command was out there to kill these men; but carrying out that kind of command has social consequences. And few were willing to actually obey—because in real life, if a person obeyed this command and killed the sinners, then he was likely killing some of his own family. That would be a heavy thing for anyone to live with. And if a person killed someone else's relatives, that group may want to seek vengeance and retaliate. And as result of this inaction, the sin continued to grow and become more blatant, and God started a plague of some kind that started wiping out a lot of Israel. It's not clear how much time elapsed between the command, the start of the plague, and the end of the plague, but verse six tells us how quickly that lust burned out of control:

> Then an Israelite man brought to his family a Midianite woman right before the eyes of Moses and the whole assembly of Israel while they were weeping at the entrance to the Tent of Meeting. When Phinehas son of Eleazar, the son of Aaron, the priest, saw this, he left the assembly, took a spear in his hand and followed the Israelite into the tent. He drove the spear through both of them—through the Israelite and into the woman's body. Then the plague against the Isra-

elites was stopped; but those who died in the plague numbered 24,000. *(Numbers 25:6-9)*

Look what that lust-filled man did. He ignored Moses. He ignored the prayer meeting and the weeping and all the people. He had no shame whatsoever as his out-of-control desires had made him blind to God and to the consequences of his sin. And he brought a foreign woman into his family tent and finally wasted no time in engaging with her, as the Bible graphically notes. I know he never, ever expected this sin to have a deadly payday.

Finally someone stepped up and said, "Enough!" It wasn't Moses; it wasn't Joshua. It was a guy named Phinehas. He had heard the command of God and watched as everyone had ignored it. He had seen the plague and still didn't do anything. But something stirred in him at the sight of this brazen act, and he finally did what everyone else should have done with him. He did what God asked, and as a result thousands were saved. What he did that day is notable. It's easy to forget that people in the Bible were real people, with skin and families and bad breath. And when I see this kind of courage in the face of fighting communal sin, I am humbled and hope to confront evil in my own life with the same kind of energy and zeal. God was so moved that Phinehas got special notation:

> The LORD said to Moses, "Phinehas son of Eleazar, the son of Aaron, the priest, has turned my anger away from the Israelites; for he was as zealous as I am for my honor among them, so that in my zeal I did

not put an end to them. Therefore tell him I am making my covenant of peace with him. He and his descendants will have a covenant of a lasting priesthood, because he was zealous for the honor of his God and made atonement for the Israelites." *(Numbers 25:10-13)*

I love verse 13 because it says, "He was zealous for the honor of his God." I want that to be said of me more often. I want to make God look good, both in my public moments on stage at my church and my private moments in my home with my wife and kids. I like that guy Phinehas.

So let me circle in for a landing and see if the connection between the stories of the prodigal son and the Moabite women in Israel have any bearing on life in our world today. I also want to look at how these two stories speak of the same God. At first glance, I didn't see the connection at all. It seemed to me that God the Father in the prodigal story was nice and merciful and that the God in Numbers was not so nice and certainly not patient with wayward kids. I feel as if I know the prodigal's father better than the God of Israel. But after further review, I'm starting to see the connection. God is the same in both places; it's the people who aren't.

Let me explain. In the prodigal story we know that the father Jesus talked about is our Heavenly Father. So the prodigal was already in the family but wanted out—he wanted to live it up and strayed. And we also know that Israel was God's chosen nation and is frequently described as His children, but they, too, wanted to stray and did so mightily. The difference between the two stories appears to be what happens when sin catches up with God's children. Israel saw the plague happening; they knew God was angry and had demanded death to the sinners and atonement for sin. But they just couldn't find the strength to turn their hearts back to God and stop sinning, even though a sex-induced plague was ravaging the community. The prodigal, however, was hit by the same truth. His sin had caught up with him. The wages of his sin were separation from his family and his father and total poverty. And that's where the stories diverge. The prodigal son turned his heart toward home and repented. The people of Israel did not, and apparently the Father knew that they would not, though His desire for His children is always life, not death. Listen to the prophet Hosea issue a plea on behalf of Father God to another wayward generation of Israelites in another time:

> Return, O Israel, to the LORD your God. Your sins have been your downfall! Take words with you and return to the LORD. Say to him: "Forgive all our sins and receive us graciously, that we may offer the fruit of our lips." *(Hosea 14:1-2)*

The God of the Old Testament is the same God in the New. He doesn't want His children to sin because it hurts Him, it hurts them, and it hurts the ones they love. Sin is a life of settling for illusion over truth, lies over love.

So let's contemporize this. Over the years I have spoken to many people who are followers of Christ but who also struggle with hidden ungodly addictions and vices. Many have just accepted these sinful behaviors as a part of life that can't be overcome this side of glory. I have a feeling that our Heavenly Father has a different take on sin, and so do I. And with nearly twenty years of Internet living, sexual sin has become more prevalent and available than ever before as the shield of privacy has lowered the normal social boundaries against such behavior. But sexual sin, as well as any other sin, is a big deal to God, no matter how small we may see it. J. C. Ryle warns us about naiveté when it comes to the monster called sin:

> I fear we do not sufficiently realize the extreme subtlety of our soul's disease. We are too apt to forget that temptation to sin will rarely present itself to us in its true colours, saying, "I am your deadly enemy and I want to ruin you forever in hell." Oh, no! Sin comes to us, like Judas, with a kiss, and like Joab, with an outstretched hand and flattering words. The forbidden fruit seemed good and desirable to Eve, yet it cast her out of Eden. The walking idly on his palace roof seemed harmless enough to David, yet it ended in adultery and murder. Sin rarely seems sin at its first beginnings. . . . We may give wickedness smooth names, but we cannot alter its nature and character in the sight of God.[1]

Let me get personal with you for a minute. No matter what anyone tells you, God knows exactly what happens in your personal Vegas. He doesn't laugh it off as human horseplay or wink at your misdeeds. He understands what you have done and continue to do. And He calls it by its right name. He understands that your sin is soul cancer and is affecting every decision you make, and most important, your relationship with Him as well. He wants to set you free because of His love for you. He knows that sin is basically self-love that deprives your soul of what it really needs. He doesn't tell any of us to quit sinning to ruin our fun. He begs us to quit sinning because it is killing us if we don't.

I want you to take a minute to say a quick prayer to God. If you have read this chapter this far, then I believe God wants to uncover an area in your life where you may be living with sin and not dealing with it. So will you just take a minute and pray this bold prayer? This is a prayer for people who want to be like Phineas—full of courage and zeal for the things of God.

Father God, search my mind and my memory. Am I deceiving myself and allowing sin in my life?

After you ask that of God, I want you to listen for His voice. Usually the first thought in your head after you pray that kind of prayer is the thing that God wants to remove first. So if you are really ready to get on with things, pray the following prayer next:

God, I see that thing, and I see that it is sin. Remove it from me. I confess it is sin and vow to avoid it, with your help, in the future. I thank you that Jesus died to forgive me of that sin and also to cleanse me of the guilt that comes with it. In Jesus' name I pray. Amen.

If you prayed that prayer, then know that our Father delights in bringing His grace to you. Listen to how God deals with His kids who come home: "I will heal their way-wardness and love them freely, for my anger has turned away from them" (Hosea 14:4). And as a New Testament believer, I understand that this healing comes from the work of Jesus Christ on the Cross. The apostle Paul affirms how we can live this way every day, even in a morally polluted world.

In the same way, count yourselves dead to sin but alive to God in Christ Jesus. Therefore do not let sin reign in your mortal body so that you obey its evil desires. Do not offer the parts of your body to sin, as instruments of wickedness, but rather offer yourselves to God, as those who have been brought from death to life; and offer the parts of your body to him as instruments of righteousness. For sin shall not be your master, because you are not under law, but under grace. *(Romans 6:11-14)*

Like the prodigal son and the nation of Israel, you and I have a choice when it comes to sin. Will you repent and choose life today? Or will you suffer at the hands of a cruel master who will eventually destroy the work of God and His good future in your life? What happens in your heart matters to God!

The last thing I want you to consider is what God told Israel after the plague was stopped.

The LORD said to Moses, "Treat the Midianites as enemies and kill them, because they treated you as enemies when they deceived you in the affair of Peor." *(Numbers 25:16-18)*

I believe our God would be delighted to see a group of people begin to hate sin as much as He does and commit to live their lives full of zeal for His honor.

Home is on the horizon for those who are ready to turn away from the self-exalting pigpens of life. But making it all the way back home will be no small task. It will take resolve and power and inner healing brought by the light of truth. This journey will also require strength and courage and humility. In fact, facing this journey alone is impossible. The only way to make it all the way back home in our world today will be through miraculous intervention by the only one who has the strength to carry us there. This next story shows us a real-life example of deliverance and homecoming.

Can You Relate?

Read through the following questions and record your thoughts and reactions.

1. Write about an area of your life where you have a "What happens in Vegas stays in Vegas" mentality. Do you compartmentalize different behaviors for different surroundings? Are there habits or friends who encourage this behavior?

_____

_____

_____

_____

_____

_____

_____

_____

_____

_____

_____

_____

_____

_____

_____

_____

2. Write about the sugary yet deadly attractants you have swallowed. Think about steps you could have taken to avoid them. In what ways have these led you to become more aware of what an attractant is? Record a time when you have fallen prey to or avoided one such attractant.

_____

_____

_____

_____

_____

_____

_____

_____

_____

_____

_____

_____

_____

_____

_____

_____

_____

_____

3. James 2:10 implies that God does not count one sin greater than any other. Have you ever been guilty of this mind-set? Explain. Do you have a tendency to prioritize, fixing sins according to this hierarchy? If so, in what ways?

_____

_____

_____

_____

_____

_____

_____

_____

_____

_____

_____

_____

_____

_____

_____

_____

4. Is the punishing side of God one you avoid thinking about? How is ignoring this side of God harmful to your relationship with Him? In what ways might it cause you to sin more or less often? What steps can you take to reconcile your opposing views of God?

_____

_____

_____

_____

_____

_____

_____

_____

_____

_____

_____

_____

_____

_____

_____

_____

_____

5. Is your reaction to God's punishment in your life more like the Israelites or the prodigal son? Do you have a hard time accepting His punishment as beneficial to you? Explain.

_____

_____

_____

_____

_____

_____

_____

_____

_____

_____

_____

_____

_____

_____

_____

_____

_____

_____

_____

6. Most find it easy to hate "big" sins like rape and murder, but do you hate "little" sins, like lying and gossip, as God does? Explain what little sins you struggle with. When it comes to others' lives and behavior, do you still see sins as little and big, or is it only in your own life that these categories exist?

_____

_____

_____

_____

_____

_____

_____

_____

_____

_____

_____

_____

_____

_____

_____

_____

THREE
THE WAY HOME

When he came to his senses, he said . . .

"I will set out and go back to my father."

—Luke 15:17-18

I don't know a lot of Scottish people. From what I have learned, they are a feisty lot with rich accents and densely patterned facial hair that makes most of us in the United States appear just a meter short of wimpy. The Scottish even seem to have a higher tolerance for pain than most, evidenced by the fact that they invented the devious pastime we now refer to as golf. It's such a sinister diversion with a tenderly benign face. It combines a beautiful piece of real estate, a simple goal, a high-tech stick, and a ball. *What could go wrong?* you ask yourself before setting out. And moments later you inevitably find yourself flung to your knees in various fits of rage, anger, and/or betrayal. Pain, thy name is golf. But by today's standards, golfing is not necessarily a "manly" sport, although many manly men love to golf, I've been told. Consider the whole idea of being quiet during backswings and wearing pastels instead of primary colors. I'm prone to believe that the Scots should have come up with something like "full-contact golf" by now if the PGA had let them.

But that's enough about the Scots. It took an Irish man to take the game of golf to the level of greatness that it enjoys today in the heartland. They tell me "Rickey" is an Irish name, by the way, so even though I admire the Scottish from afar, I'm in hip-deep with the men from the green land. The Irish man I have in mind was my kind of golfer. His name was Mulligan. Do you hear the richness in that name? It just rolls off the tongue, especially when you try it with an Irish brogue. Go ahead and try it—I'll wait.

Mulligan must have been an average golfer who loved the idea of grace. (I have not done any research to verify this statement, so these details may or may not be true about him.) But what a guy he was, that Mulligan! Even today his name is bantered about on tee boxes all over the world. You see, the word "mulligan" has even become a noun. And in golfing parlance, mulligan literally means "do-over." As in, if you hit a bad golf shot, you take a mulligan, and you swing again without any penalty. It's as if that first ball you hit into the woods never existed or as if that drive you sunk into the pond at hole eighteen literally went into the "sea of forgetfulness." I like to golf with people who let me take as many mulligans as I need. I call it "amazing grace" golf. You would expect that kind of talk from a pastor, wouldn't you?

I think I'm in good company here when I speak of "do-overs" in life. Jesus seemed to like mulligans too, but His kinds of mulligans aren't golf-related. Think back to our prodigal story. The younger brother was in a bad place—deep weeds, if you will. His life had gone out of bounds. He was hungry and frustrated by his errant shots at greatness, and he needed a fresh start. And the four simple words that we learn from the younger brother are life-changing for all of us who have made bad shots in life. The four words are simple: You can begin again.

I learned this fact most vividly by a particular Bible story that seems strange to modern sensibilities. It involves Jesus and a man who was living off course and on the fringe of society. We never learn his name, but we do learn about his issues. And in the end of his story we are brought face to face with the freshness and healing power found in the wonderful grace of Jesus. Here's how the disciple Mark describes things:

> They [Jesus and the disciples] went across the lake to the region of the Gerasenes. When Jesus got out of the boat, a man with an evil spirit came from the tombs to meet him. This man lived in the tombs, and no one could bind him any more, not even with a chain. For he had often been chained hand and foot, but he tore the chains apart and broke the irons on his feet. No one was strong enough to subdue him. Night and day among the tombs and in the hills he would cry out and cut himself with stones. *(Mark 5:1-5)*

How's that for a greeting? You get out of your boat and onto land, still trying to get the mud out of your toes because you're wearing old-school sandals, and a crazy man steps up to say hello. The hair was likely standing up on the back of the disciples' necks. Not only was this dirty, creepy guy one brick shy of a full load, but he also had spiritual issues that made him dangerous. Horror movies borrow from the reality in this scene, and I guarantee you that you and I would have wanted to leave that beach quickly. But Jesus wasn't scared. Creepy people never did bother Him. What we call "creepy" Jesus called *opportunity*. What an optimist Jesus was! He saw something nobody else saw. In fact, three things stood out about the man.

First, he was in chains. The story tells us that someone had tried to bind him with chains, but they couldn't. The fact that he was in chains shows us that he had a penchant for doing the wrong thing. Whether it was theft, vandalism, rape, or murder, we don't know. But what we do know is that the evil in his heart had found its way into evil activity. And that evil was truly powerful. Although he broke the chains on his body, the chains on his heart were too strong for him to break on his own.

I have had the opportunity to speak with many people who are facing these kinds of inner chains. I remember speaking to one man about his marriage. He recounted to me that a few years previous, his wife had decided to stray. The ensuing problems led them to file for divorce, but they could not go through with it. They decided to reconcile and learn firsthand how to apply God's grace to their marriage. But even though he had vocalized his forgiveness and was doing his best, he was still having problems feeling free. He was chained to memories and knowledge that he desperately wanted to lose. You don't have to be a crazy man to have chains.

As I write this book, many in my area are facing home foreclosure following job losses that they simply can't recover from. They have the heavy chains of debt that they are unable to shake off. Others are fighting the feelings of worthlessness that come from prolonged unemployment. Chains come in all shapes and all sizes, but as we shall see in a moment, chains are not any match for Jesus.

The second thing that stands out about the lost man in the story is that he was beyond hope. Verse 4 says, "No one was strong enough to subdue him." He was obviously strong and dangerous. No one felt safe with him around. The best place for him seemed to be a sort of self-imposed solitary confinement. It's amazing that in our culture the prison population continues to explode with these same kinds of men and women. For whatever reason, we seem to think that placing a person in a box like an animal for long periods of time will make him or her somehow less like an animal. This man didn't have hope for his future, because he didn't have a future. And scores in our prisons today are facing the same bleak hopelessness. They know what it's like to feel forgotten and disposable.

Let me ask a quick question as an aside: Why do you think more Christians don't visit those who live in prison? I know the answer is simply ignorance, or worse, comfort and convenience, but consider this: in His parable of the sheep and the goats, Jesus condemned people who claim to be Christians who do not engage in this simple act of social justice. In Matthew 25 Jesus told a parable of contrast starring sheep (the redeemed) and goats (those doomed for destruction.) In describing the goats and the reason they would not experience eternal reward, He said, "For I was hungry and you gave me nothing to eat, I was thirsty and you gave me nothing to drink, I was a stranger and you did not invite me in, I needed clothes and you did not clothe me, I was sick and in prison and you did not look after me" (Matthew 25:42-43). The fact that Jesus left thousands of people on the other side of the lake to tend to this one individual ought to give us a clue of how badly we're missing the boat in this instance.

I've seen prison ministry work well. In Tulsa, Oklahoma, I was able to lead a church that attempted to do this each week as a part of worship. The law in Oklahoma allows certain minimum security prisoners to go to church on weekends provided the prisoners have a sponsor to watch over them and get them back at night. So initially we had one guy who felt a burden to help these inmates get to church. We bought a short bus, and very quickly he filled it with guys who attended our Saturday night and Sunday morning services. Soon after that, God provided a big bus for us that they were able to fill up each week with up to sixty guys. These were guys that were in pain and in chains but were now getting to experience true freedom in Christ, even while they were still incarcerated. When I left Tulsa in January 2009, ten former inmates were regular members of the church, living on the outside. All this was possible because somebody said, "The Bible says we should take care of the prisoners, Pastor." And they were right. So we did, and Jesus jumped in and did the heavy lifting of changing their lives.

But let me get back to the scary man in the story. The third thing that stands out to me is that he was in terrible pain. Look at verse five again. "Night and day among the tombs and in the hills he would cry out and cut himself with stones."

He may have been physically strong, but on the inside he was just plain brokenhearted. I know that he probably suffered at least three kinds of pain common in our day as well.

The first was the pain of isolation. Nobody invited him to dinner or to game night or to the camel races. I'm sure somebody had tried along the way, but it just didn't work. Currently the United States population exceeds 308 million people and is growing. But even with all the people living around us, loneliness is a terrible disease affecting more and more every day.[1]

I'm sure he also felt the pain of hopelessness. He was a person who was certainly at the point he could no longer help himself. In the prison ministry I spoke of earlier, I had the chance to hear the stories of men locked into the hopelessness of addiction to methamphetamine or crystal meth. Meth addiction is a problem affecting more and more families, both upper and lower class, and it is literally filling up our prisons. It's the kind of drug that many have told me is instantly addictive, because the high lasts up to ten times as long as cocaine and feels even more powerful. A friend of mine who had been clean for a number of years called it "the devil in powdered form."

The men I spoke to talked of the constant battle that went on in their minds. On one hand, in their clearer moments they knew that meth was wrong and that it was bad for their future. But the desire for the drug inside them was many times stronger than their desire to quit. Many times they failed in their battle to overcome their addictions. And many times relapse caused them to quit the recovery program all together. This would land them back in the cycle of hopelessness. They longed to be free but didn't have the strength to break the chains of addiction.

I believe the man in the story likely had another source of pain. This isn't in the text, but I've found that people this broken almost always suffer from the pain of bitterness. I'm sure that in his mind everybody had done him wrong. He had probably played the blame game and come to the conclusion that everyone else had the problem, not him. This is one of the devil's biggest tricks—to entice men and women to live in the past and harbor resentment against everybody. And when a person harbor's resentment against a lot of people, they eventually find themselves floating through life alone.

But the story isn't over. Look at what happens next.

When he saw Jesus from a distance, he ran and fell on his knees in front of him. He shouted at the top of his voice, "What do you want with me, Jesus, Son of the Most High God? Swear to God that you won't torture me!" For Jesus had said to him, "Come out of this man, you evil spirit!" Then Jesus asked him, "What is your name?" "My name is Legion," he replied, "for we are many." And he begged Jesus again and again not to send them out of the area. A large herd of pigs was feeding on the nearby hillside. The demons begged Jesus, "Send us among the pigs; allow us to go into them." He gave them permission, and the evil spirits came out and went into the pigs. The herd, about two thousand in number, rushed down the steep bank into the lake and was drowned. *(Mark 5:6-13)*

Let me summarize: this horrible man with all these demonic issues, addictions, hurts, and pain finally gets to see Jesus. And when he sees Jesus, he has a moment of clarity. I know this, because I see it in his response to Jesus. Look back at verse 6: "When he saw Jesus from a distance, he ran and fell on his knees in front of him."

For me, this is one of the coolest events in all of Scripture, because it's one of the few times we get to see a detailed, real-life portrait of a person before and after accepting Jesus. And even though he was rotten to the core and overflowing with demons, he still ran to Jesus and fell on his knees. He had tried everything else. He knew he was hopeless. He was broken. He had injured himself over and over. He cried out all the time. He was disposable, and he was forgotten. He was forgotten by everyone not named Jesus, that is. And when he saw Jesus, he ran. He didn't walk. He didn't look back. He ran face-forward and knelt at the feet of the answer to his pain.

So how did he know Jesus could help him? That is the question, isn't it? The text doesn't provide us a clear answer, so I'm going to use some experiential language from the way Jesus still heals broken people today and make a few logical jumps. You can disagree with me, but you can't prove me wrong either. I believe that when he saw Jesus, he was compelled or called to come and kneel. Nobody heard the call out loud. There was no audible voice from heaven, but I believe in his heart he felt this call. It's a call that he may have felt before and ignored, but never this intense. So why do you suppose he was able to accept this unspoken call this time?

Here's what I believe. First, I believe he sensed the unconditional love of Jesus. This man had not seen real love in a long time. He was a throwaway. Yet there was something about Jesus that made him run toward Him, not away. Many people today run from Jesus because they don't really understand His love. And just like this man, they are living captive to the lies of the enemy. But this man had heard enough of the lies in his head. He knew he couldn't get better on his own, and he wanted some kind of normal life again. And over to his personal graveyard walked Jesus. The fact that Jesus was walking in his direction and not ignoring him may have been the first act of kindness this man had seen in a while.

I think sometimes all of us underestimate the power of kindness. Sometimes when I watch cable television and they have a "religious" representative on air to comment, I get a little sick to my stomach. From the outside, it can seem as if Christians have red faces and like to fight a lot, just like the guy I mentioned in chapter one from Starbucks. I know this isn't true of all Christians, but I really wish many Christians would just learn to be nicer. Kindness is more powerful in promoting change than arguing, or demeaning other persons' views. In fact, kindness is God's favorite tactic in bringing about what He wants done in the world. In Romans, Paul wrote, "Do you not realize that God's kindness is meant to lead you to repentance?" (Romans 2:4 NRSV). And when Jesus paid attention to this guy instead of ignoring him, He was showing concern. Real love always pays attention.

Not only was the scary man able to sense the love of Jesus—he also sensed the power that Jesus carried with Him. Verse 6 says that "He fell on his knees." It's one thing to feel loved by someone, but he also perceived that Jesus could actually fix him. He knew that he was powerless to change on his own, and now he was meeting a person of power. He knew he himself didn't have the answers inside.

Many good people today fail at this point when it comes to Jesus. They treat Him like a good buddy to talk with, or like the AAA man who gets them out of periodic jams—but not like a God to be worshiped. I'm not sure how or why this happens, but I know I've been guilty of this myself. When I pray, I know Jesus is listening and that He is my friend, but sometimes I really don't think of Him as the all-powerful Creator of the universe that He is. I just don't picture Jesus with the strength and ability that He alone possesses. I just forget. As a result, my prayers can become formulaic. I pray because I know I should, but not because I believe Jesus will actually do anything about it.

It's not always this way for me. Sometimes I get a clear line with heaven and know God is going to answer, but those times are more infrequent than they should be. Jesus has the power to change anything and everything. I know this in my head, but sometimes I don't act like it. Sound like anyone you know? I'm glad that this man was able to see the power available in Jesus. It's a great reminder for any of us who struggle with faith from time to time.

After he acknowledged the power of Jesus, he was able to experience the freedom that only Jesus can give. Look at verse 13: "The evil spirits came out." Now that had to feel good when those demons left the scene. The feeling of freedom suddenly gave his life meaning. The pain was over. The peace of God rushed in to replace the pain of confusion. The addiction to Jesus began, and the addiction to evil was broken. A new future appeared from the ashes of his life, and his hopelessness was gone. Jesus gave this young man a startling reminder that the demons that once held him captive were gone for good. The visual comes as the pigs, filled with demons, decided that suicide was better than life with demons inside.

In one of the greatest stories of transformation we find in the Bible, Jesus shouts one simple fact to anyone who will listen: *You can begin again!* You can have real freedom from your past, your pain, and your hurts.

Have you ever had your back adjusted by a chiropractor? He or she does this pushing thing and this twisting thing, and then the pain leaves. Feels good, doesn't it? It feels like freedom. The devil's purpose for this guy's life was to steal, to kill, and destroy. Before he met Jesus, he was in chains. He was beyond hope, and he was in terrible pain. But when He saw Jesus, I know he sensed the love of Jesus, the power of Jesus, and the freedom.

This same Jesus will come to anyone who is dealing with brokenness, bitterness, betrayal, hopelessness, worry, loneliness, and frustration. He comes to anyone who will look for Him and listen to His voice of love. And when Jesus comes, He comes in power, with His power that is able to set a person free from any of the bondage of the past or the brokenness of the present. When Jesus sets someone free as only He can, the person then knows the reality of His words "If the Son sets you free, you will be free indeed!" (John 8:36).

As you read this, I want you to let this get personal. How are things in your heart right now? Are you hiding or running from Jesus, or are things super? Are you feeling "free indeed" or burdened by a lot of things? Maybe you weren't even aware of it until now. But remember this story. This guy had a life before Jesus, but it got better after he brought his issues to Jesus.

Some of you who read this may not know that you could be whole again. You may have tried to get fixed or have a better life only to fall back into the same old patterns of failure. The simple truth is this: no matter who you are, you can begin again. If you have gone through a painful divorce, you can begin again. If you have abandoned your family, you can begin again. If you are now in prison, you can begin again. If you have cheated on your taxes or stolen from your employer, you can begin again. If you have betrayed a close friend and have lost everything or everyone you ever cared about, you can begin again. The key to beginning again won't be found in an old pair of pants or underneath the couch. The key to new beginnings is always found in Jesus Christ alone.

Jesus calls out to all of us, as part of broken humanity, with this simple good news message: "Follow me; I have a better way to live. I will give you the peace you lack and the joy you are chasing. I am your answer. It comes from me, and in me. I want you to commit to me, because I am committed to you." I don't think the world outside the Church understands this message of love and power. I wish they did. I hope they will.

I know that many inside the Church don't understand this message of transformation. They invite Jesus to help them in their messy lives, but they don't want Him to change it too much. They want Jesus as Savior to get them out of trouble, but not really as the Lord who calls the shots. I've found that Jesus will only be a person's Lord and Savior. It's His pick.

So let's put a bow on this story. After Jesus came all the way across the lake for this one person, and after He changed this guy's life completely, He turned around and decided to leave as quickly as he had come.

As Jesus was getting into the boat, the man who had been demon-possessed begged to go with Him. Jesus did not let him but instead said, "'Go home to your family and tell them how much the Lord has done for you, and how he has had mercy on you.' So the man went away and began to tell in the Decapolis how much Jesus had done for him. And all the people were amazed." *(Mark 5:18-20)*

Jesus left the man, but on the way out He gave an order. He told the man to "go . . . and tell." So the man "went . . . and began to tell." After the healing the message got recycled. The pain was used to bring God glory, and the scripture says the people were amazed—all of them.

People in the recovery movement understand this point better than most. They understand that the healing power of God continues inside a person as he or she shares the story of deliverance to others. There is healing in transparency, just as there is harm in self-righteous denial.

Think about this man's life after the healing. He had to get a job; he had to make amends to the people he had hurt. He had to regain his family's trust all over again, and by all means he had to keep telling others. The day he met Jesus for real, his eternal life began, and it was a different kind of life. Peter affirms that "Your new life is not like your old life" (1 Peter 1:23, TM).

He didn't wait to get to heaven to live eternally; he got heaven on earth. And just like this man, Jesus wants to save us from living for ourselves to living for someone greater. We are given eternal life now to share. The man Jesus healed was different, not just forgiven. And he was given a new plan for his future. This story is not just a picture of a life nearly two thousand years ago—it's a picture of your life and my life before and after Jesus.

The younger son in the prodigal story had reached bottom. Like the demoniac, he couldn't help himself any longer. He knew the way back home, and he humbly took it. The party that followed is legendary.

Is there something holding you back from God today? I certainly hope not, especially after reading this great story of redemption and transformation. Remember: no matter who you are, and no matter what you have done, mulligans are available to you. They are a gift of grace that Jesus paid for on the Cross. He has guaranteed that our sins can be forgiven, that our hearts can be cleansed, and that we can be granted a new start. All one has to do is to do is ask. It is good news, isn't it? Makes you smile a little, doesn't it? Sometimes it's good to be at the bottom, because the only direction to look is up.

Can You Relate?

Read through the following questions and record your thoughts and reactions.

1. In what areas of your life could you use mulligans? Philippians 4:13 says "I can do everything through him who gives me strength." Have you ever received a mulligan but not taken this verse to heart and needed another mulligan? Do you truly believe that when you live this verse out, mulligans will no longer be necessary? Explain.

_____

_____

_____

_____

_____

_____

_____

_____

_____

_____

_____

_____

_____

_____

_____

2. How would you immediately react to a man like the possessed one in the story? Would you have been like the disciples, scared to death, or like Jesus, immediately willing to help? In light of the above verse, would you change your answer?

_____

_____

_____

_____

_____

_____

_____

_____

_____

_____

_____

_____

_____

_____

_____

_____

_____

3. Is there a difference between helping someone in physical chains and helping someone in spiritual chains? Do you agree that both situations can cause hopelessness and the feeling that you are forgotten and disposable? In what ways?

_____

_____

_____

_____

_____

_____

_____

_____

_____

_____

_____

_____

_____

_____

_____

_____

_____

_____

4. Do you find yourself blaming others for tough situations you're in? Is there a person in particular you tend to blame for your circumstances? Are there any situations you are particularly bitter about? What are the common denominators?

_____

_____

_____

_____

_____

_____

_____

_____

_____

_____

_____

_____

_____

_____

_____

_____

_____

_____

5. Describe how you visualize Jesus. Now think of a time when things were going wrong in your life. Did He look different then? How about a time when things were going well? Did your style of prayer differ in these times?

_____

_____

_____

_____

_____

_____

_____

_____

_____

_____

_____

_____

_____

_____

_____

_____

_____

6. "There is healing in transparency," not just for you but also for those around you. What is your personal testimony? How many times have you shared your testimony? What is hindering you from doing so more often? Are you embarrassed by your life prior to salvation, or do you feel your story is not important enough to share? Explain.

_____

_____

_____

_____

_____

_____

_____

_____

_____

_____

_____

_____

_____

_____

_____

_____

SECTION TWO

Lost Inside
(Oldest Son)

FOUR
SETTLING ACCOUNTS

On the judgment day, fire will reveal what
kind of work each builder has done. The fire will
show if a person's work has any value.

—1 Corinthians 3:13, NLT

Fire comes in human packages sometimes.

When I was eight years old, my parents had one of those ideas that end up changing a lot of lives forever while bringing a bit of fire. At this point in my life, I was settled into my role as the only child at home. My three older siblings had already left the nest years before and were now enjoying their own families. At home I was the king of my little kingdom. I could eat all the Pop-Tarts if I wanted to. Nobody else liked my favorite cereal. I could read or play ball without giving a thought to anybody else and get up late on Saturdays and watch the cartoons I wanted to watch. I have long asked the question, "Why would anybody want to mess up such a great thing for me?" This was the time in my life that I learned that things really weren't all about me. It was not a lesson I learned very quickly, however.

My parents, Norman and Eloise, always had this nagging habit of following the voice of God as they understood it. This was a good habit when things went my preferred way. But the decision they made to invite a stranger into our home was not really what I had in mind. His name was Chris. His function in my life was to become "the fire."

Chris was a six-year-old boy with olive skin and small bones and a crooked little devilish smile. He was in our Michigan church, living in foster care with a lovely family in our congregation. The people he was staying with were the kind, quiet, thoughtful types who could have posed for a Norman Rockwell family portrait. And Chris would have been the one in the photo holding up two fingers to make rabbit ears over his sister's head, with his semi-forked tongue sticking out.

I had first noticed Chris at church weeks before my parents' landmark decision. He was the boy who never sat down when the teacher was speaking. He loved all the attention, was very disruptive, and couldn't be still for more than ten seconds. He was that kid.

So imagine my surprise when my parents had "the talk" with me to explain they felt that they wanted to add another person to our three-bedroom home, just for now, to try out the idea of adoption. Shock number one came because I was the king, and they were in effect dethroning me from my rightful position. I was the fourth-born but the one and only kid at home. I had rights! The real shock came when they named the suspect. I say "suspect" because I believed that I was witnessing a crime against my humanity. I'm not sure what or who I was prepared for, but it was not the one they picked. I said, "Chris? Really? No, you have to be joking!" I ran into the kitchen and checked the calendar; it wasn't April 1. It was not a joke. They had heard from God, and they were listening. But I was not in the mood to get spiritual. For many years I was never, ever in the mood for Chris.

When Chris came into our home, I didn't give him much of a chance. I tried a little, but our personalities conflicted immediately. He was a normal kid with high emotional needs brought on by his difficult early life. It wasn't his fault he was born into a highly dysfunctional home where addiction was a way of life. He wanted to be a part of a family, and he should have been welcomed, but I didn't have room in my heart. He wanted to be friends with my friends, play ball when I played ball, and eat the same Pop-Tarts I ate—until they were gone. I finally concluded that I just wanted to be left alone. But Chris never did leave me alone. He just wanted to be included. He wanted to have a life and a family like normal people. These were the years when our family began to understand the fact that following the voice of God does not mean it will be the easy way to go. Nothing about being with Chris was ever easy in those early years. Fire is usually hot up close; and it was too close.

When I was ten, we moved out of state and had to make a family decision. My parents concluded that Chris was their child, and he was legally adopted into our family. He still carries the same last name and has all the rights as the youngest son of Norman and Eloise. But making this adoption official still made no dent in my hardening heart. Chris and I coexisted throughout our school years, but I wouldn't say we ever loved one another.

Thankfully, that came later. But throughout our difficult years at home, I fought the urge to question my parent's judgment. On one side, I understood that the Bible commands us to care for the widows and orphans (Isaiah 1:17). But on the other side, I didn't like what Chris had pulled out of me. I didn't like the mean boy that I had become to him. I didn't like the fact that I bullied him and put him down. And it was just plain easier to blame my parents than to take responsibility for being a sinner who needed God's love and needed to learn how to love others. The refiner was working on me to teach me how to love.

The Older Brother

In the story of the prodigal son, the older brother doesn't come off looking very good. In fact, after reading it closely, one can see that the older brother is just as lost as the younger brother. The younger brother was wild and crazy and never cared about anyone but himself. But the older brother was blind and selfish and judgmental. He, too, was more concerned for himself than anyone else. And being a recovering older brother myself, I fully understand where the guy was coming from when he didn't really want the younger son back in the house. He had things the way he wanted them without interruption. He didn't have to share his Pop-Tarts and was happy about it. He had earned the right for the party. He didn't want to carve up his estate any more than he already had. I'm learning that sharing is always hardest on people who are addicted to having more.

Grace is always great for the receiver, isn't it? But grace is a bit of a scandal for those on the other end who watch the grace being given. See—the kingdom of this world demands justice and pay-for-service. But the kingdom of God works through mercy and grace. Jesus told another parable that highlighted our innate problem with grace and His great desire to give it away.

The kingdom of heaven is like a landowner who went out early in the morning to hire men to work in his vineyard. He agreed to pay them a denarius for the day and sent them into his vineyard. About the third hour he went out and saw others standing in the marketplace doing nothing. He told them, "You also go and work in my vineyard, and I will pay you whatever is right." So they went. He went out again about the sixth hour and the ninth hour and did the same thing. About the eleventh hour he went out and found still others standing around. He asked them, "Why have you been standing here all day long doing nothing?" "Because no one has hired us," they answered. He said to them, "You also go and work in my vineyard." When evening came, the owner of the vineyard said to his foreman, "Call the workers and pay them their wages, beginning with the last ones hired and going on to the first." The workers who were hired about the eleventh hour came and each received a denarius. So when those came who were hired first, they expected to receive more. But each one of them also received a denarius. When they received it, they began to grumble against the landowner. "These men who were hired last worked only one hour," they said, "and you have made them equal to us who have borne the burden of the work and the heat of the day." But he answered one of them, "Friend, I am not being unfair to you. Didn't you agree to work for a denarius? Take your pay and go. I want to give the man who was hired last the same as I gave you. Don't I have the right to do what I want with my own money? Or are you envious because I am generous?" So the last will be first, and the first will be last. *(Matthew 20:1-16)*

Now for any who have adopted a pay-for-service, earn-your-way-through-life mentality, this is really an outrageous story. It doesn't even have an element of fairness or justice to it. It is unfair and unjust, at least to those hired early on. I instantly identify with the workers chosen in the morning crew, and I would have been the first to complain at the inequity. I would be willing to bet that most of the people I know would share my grievance. And this feeling is why so many people have a problem with God. Many good people like the idea of God's grace on the front end, just like the workers who got hired in the morning. They were likely happy at the outset and satisfied to be among those the landowner had chosen. And they expect him to reward them based on a sliding scale according to their level of sacrifice and obedience. Unfortunately, the phrase "You get what you pay for" has made its way into our theology.

I notice three things about God's grace in this story that sometimes, in my weaker moments, apply to me.

First, I love the idea of God's grace. The landowner in this parable gets up early and looks for people who will serve, and he promises a fair reward. Notice that the landowner was looking for helpers. But they weren't necessarily looking for him. In theological terms, this is a picture of God's prevenient grace. Prevenient grace is the grace God bestowed on me that enabled me to see my need for Him before I was even a believer. Without God's prevenient grace, my sinful heart would never have been able to see His free offer of saving grace. The landowner was seeking others before they were seeking him. He had a reward in mind, and he had work for them to accomplish. All they had to do was agree to the offer. The workers hired in the morning were happy people. They were selected and said yes. Imagine being a worker hired at 5 P.M. You will work only one hour but get paid for twelve. What a deal! I think I could sell that kind of job to anyone. From a distance, I love this story for their sakes; I also identify with the morning hires. But I really do love the idea of God's grace.

Second, I love the idea of God's grace—as long as I'm in charge. So do I really love the idea of God's grace if none of the benefits match up to the sacrificial input on my end? Am I really okay with a life of suffering and difficulty as a Christian when my other Christian brothers and sisters seem never to have a problem? I think I see now that I really love the idea of God's grace as long as things are going well for me. But when things are going well for others and not for me, I think I get a little ticked off at God—because He's not playing by my grace rules. And like a typical older brother or a tired vineyard worker, Peter had a problem with God's grace too.

One of the final scenes the Bible gives us of the resurrected Jesus is a day at the beach, recorded in the Book of John. Jesus cooked a meal for His boys and then taught them a lesson on the seeming arbitrary nature of God's grace. Jesus told Peter that he was in for some tough times ahead, and Peter wanted a little controlled justice. Jesus said,

> "I tell you the truth, when you were younger you dressed yourself and went where you wanted; but when you are old you will stretch out your hands, and someone else will dress you and lead you where you do not want to go." Jesus said this to indicate the kind of death by which Peter would glorify God. Then he said to him, "Follow me!" Peter turned and saw that the disciple whom Jesus loved was following them. (This was the one who had leaned back against Jesus at the supper and had said, "Lord, who is going to betray you?") When Peter saw him, he asked, "Lord, what about him?" Jesus answered, "If I want him to remain alive until I return, what is that to you? You must follow me." *(John 21:18-22)*

"Lord, what about him?" In other words, as long as I'm in hot water, I want company. Peter wanted to know that he wasn't going to be the only one; he wanted fairness and equality. But the kingdom of heaven is not based on a system of justice and rewards for service.

If you are in any kind of Christian service, especially in full-time paid ministry, this is one of the biggest obstacles you will face when it comes to God's grace. As servants of Christ, it's easy to get caught up in how hard you are working for Him and the amount of fruit that your particular tree or vine or field seems to be bearing. All is well when the tree is full and the fields are ripe, when the output equals and surpasses the input, when you see the fruits of your labors and God seems to bless the harvest abundantly beyond what was planted. Those are seasons of great grace. All feels right in the world. Seeds sown, harvest reaped in excess. God is good! And if your ministry has always had a great harvest, hang on. There are other seasons of grace ahead that may "lead you where you do not want to go."

I have watched most of the men in my family pursue careers in ministry. From their experiences, I can tell you that nearly everyone is likely to draw a tough assignment from God where the ground becomes harder to plow—a place where the seeds sown seem to never take root and fruit is harder to find; where the same techniques that brought fruit in the past only produce thorns and thistles. It is at this point, like Peter, that any of us may be prone to look at our lot and scream, "Hey! What about him? This isn't fair, and it isn't fun anymore." See—I like the idea of God's grace, as long as my good deeds place me in charge of my destiny. I have a harder time with it when things are out of my control.

I love the idea of God's grace as long as I'm in charge—and hopefully doesn't cost me too much. The older son in the prodigal story didn't want the younger son to be blessed and restored by a depletion of his savings. He may, in fact, have wanted his brother to be blessed, but not on his dime.

That was me. In my early years of growing up, when I saw families caring for orphaned children in our church, I liked the idea on the surface. I thought it was great that

90

somebody would be so kind as to give a home to a child who was previously homeless. Everybody deserves a place called home. I even put myself in an orphan's shoes, and I thought what it would be like to sleep in a dorm with other kids with no place to call home. I was sad for the orphans, which was made all the more realistic after seeing the play *Oliver!* at a local high school. The main character in that story was Charles Dickens' Oliver Twist, the lovable orphan who wanted more out of life.

So in theory I liked adoption, but I didn't like it much when it cost me something. And it cost me a great deal on the surface. Life was not as happy by any stretch with a little brother. It was hard. Because of God's grace to Chris through my parents, I got meaner. I had territory to guard now, and I didn't like competition.

As the years went by, though, and after I had moved out on my own, I realized that God's extension of grace to Chris, my younger brother, was really an extension of grace to me. I was a good kid before Chris, but I was never tested. God gave me a brother like Chris to teach me about life. He gave me a brother like Chris to try to teach me more about giving grace. He gave me a brother like Chris to remind me that the world is broken and is breaking little children as a result. Chris was literally given a shot at life in our home that he may have never received without it. God gave me a brother like Chris to show me the real meaning of the word "love" and how to apply it when I don't feel it.

My brother, Chris, is my real brother. And he would be the first to tell you that his life is still not easy. I know looking back that God was teaching me the greatest lesson He could ever teach me. He was teaching me that love is never easy, that love is in fact a choice you make. He taught me that His grace extends to others just as much as it does to me and that His grace is costly. He paid a great price to give that grace to us and asks us to share it without reserve.

So what about you? What if the greatest hardship you are facing is actually God's greatest act of grace toward you? Don't get stuck on the idea that grace will never cost you anything. It will always cost you something you feel you deserve. But if you wait long enough, you will discover the blessings that come by giving far outweigh the blessings that you store. I learned a good lesson about blessings from a couple of vultures a while back. Let me tell you about it.

Can You Relate?

Read through the following questions and record your thoughts and reactions.

1. If Brett had reacted positively to his family's adoption of Chris, how would things have been different? Was Brett's reaction necessary to cause change in his life, or could a positive outlook have caused just as much change in his life? Have you experienced a similar situation in your own life?

_____

_____

_____

_____

_____

_____

_____

_____

_____

_____

_____

_____

_____

_____

2. In what areas of your life do you consider yourself to be "king"? Brett wouldn't have been the king if it weren't for the fact that his siblings were so much older; what makes you the king in those areas of your life? Have you inherited your royalty? If you've worked for what you have, where did you get the abilities to accomplish what you did? Did anyone help you get where you are today?

_____

_____

_____

_____

_____

_____

_____

_____

_____

_____

_____

_____

_____

_____

_____

_____

_____

3. Discuss a time when your castle has been set on fire. Think of one positive experience and one negative experience with fire.

_____

_____

_____

_____

_____

_____

_____

_____

_____

_____

_____

_____

_____

_____

_____

_____

_____

_____

_____

4. The title of this chapter is "Settling Accounts." If Brett and Chris settled up, who do you think would end up owing the other? Who do you owe in your life? Have you contributed something to theirs?

_____

_____

_____

_____

_____

_____

_____

_____

_____

_____

_____

_____

_____

_____

_____

_____

_____

_____

_____

_____

5. Does it require more grace to forgive the older or younger son? Which son does your behavior more closely resemble?

_____

_____

_____

_____

_____

_____

_____

_____

_____

_____

_____

_____

_____

_____

_____

_____

_____

6. Describe a time long ago that was trying. Has the distance of time given you a better perspective? What was stopping you from seeing that fact then?

_____

_____

_____

_____

_____

_____

_____

_____

_____

_____

_____

_____

_____

_____

_____

_____

_____

_____

_____

FIVE

THE TWO VULTURES

*The older brother became angry and
refused to go in. So his father went out
and pleaded with him.*

—Luke 15:28

Yesterday I was driving down the road and saw two black vultures. Just the word "vulture" conjures up scary images, doesn't it? In Florida they have a number of birds that are just plain big, and the black vulture is one of them. If you hit one with your car, it may do some damage to the undercarriage. They possess steely black eyes and a curved, razor-sharp beak made for tearing flesh right off the bone. The beasts give a look that says, "Slow down too long in my area, and you will be my lunch as well—ha ha ha!"

So these two hungry-looking vultures were staring at some steaming road kill from the grassy knoll just off the road. The traffic had kept them pushed away from the asphalt, but not too far away. I'm sure these seasoned vultures had played this dance of chicken with Toyotas and Hondas many times before. I know their beaks had to be watering as the bloody carcass looked fresh. It was a good day to be a vulture.

Suddenly there was a break in the traffic, and out they went. One peck and a big tug brought a beef-jerky-size hunk of meat dangling out of the mouth of the first one. But the second one hung back. Another peck and another chunk by number one, but still no movement from number two, just a nervous head bob and a hesitating move forward. About that time, a car came quickly toward them, and then another, followed by long line of traffic. Knowing their moment had passed them by, they both flew away from the feast. The first one left with a good taste in his mouth, the second with a stomach full of missed opportunity.

Like those vultures, it appears to me that there are two kinds of people in our world today: those who seize the offer of the Father's graciousness and dive in and make the best of life as it comes—and those who are presented with the same options but hesitate and miss their opportunity.

The older son had an option the moment his father began to grill out with the fattened calf. Do I join this bunch and eat up? Or should I sulk outside, feasting at the table of bitterness, and show the old man what a big mistake he made? I know in my life I have taken both of those roads at different times.

This is the same option the Father presents to all of us each day. He is repeatedly showering blessings and grace our way, beginning with the beauty of the sunrise—and He constantly makes the implicit offer that subliminally asks humanity, "Will you enjoy my feast of life or will you miss out?" In reply there are two groups: those who dive in and receive His gifts with contentment and joy, and the others who miss their opportunity, stare at their blessings, and never dive in and explore God's best. But what caught my eye in writing this chapter was how the father "pleaded" with the older son.

He pleaded.

As a father, I have made these kinds of pleas to my girls on different occasions. I remember when my oldest, Jessica, was four years old, and she hated to take medicine for frequent coughs. I would do anything I could to get her to swallow the magic red syrup.

I tried the soft talk: "Honey, this will really help. Be a good girl, and take your medicine." That worked only on the first try. After she was wise to the aftertaste, I had to use different tactics.

After the soft approach had run its course and failed, I took the I'm-your-father-and-you-will-take-this-now approach. Her lips would usually purse as if they were being controlled by an unseen vice that was slowly clamping shut.

Then it usually came down to "Mindy, you hold her head, and I'll pry her mouth open with my fingers and get this in there somehow."

Love finds a way, they say. For those of you without children, ask around. You'll find that this method is neither cruel nor inhuman but rather most common in the parenting playbook.

But the most vivid picture I remember that happened on more than one occasion was watching Jessica not swallowing the red stuff but allowing it to run out of the corners of her crying mouth. The dye instantly stained her pajamas, which made her mother less than happy, and she was quickly whisked to bed in her new night-nights to sob herself to sleep.

When it says that the father "pleaded" with the older son, I think I get it. He was pleading with his son to do what would ultimately be in his own best interest. The father knew the older son had a problem with the younger, and he knew why. But the father also knew the older son had a problem with the way he ran the house. And it shows in the way he answers his father in an unfiltered moment of honesty.

Thinking of filters, one of the coolest parts about being a parent of a young child is that the child has not learned to filter his or her responses to questions about how he or she really feels. If you ask what your child thinks of Granny's apple cobbler, for instance, get ready for the truth as he or she sees it, not the sugar-coated half-truths he or she will learn as an adult. And I just like to be around little people who speak their mind. I was the same kind of honest kid for my parents. I remember my mom asking me point blank one day, "Don't you want to give your grandma a kiss?" My instant response was "No!" I'm sure my face said the same thing.

My granny knew a few things about young boys, however, and she kept moving closer anyway. I looked at her wrinkly skin, held my breath, pursed my lips, and, as I remember now as I look back on it again, it was over with very little pain. But my response to my parents that day was the honest truth. I didn't want to kiss my granny or anybody else for that matter. Kissing was for sissies, in my mind anyway.

As I grew up I learned that such displays of honesty are sometimes dangerous. People want to hear that you're fine when they ask how you're doing today. They don't want the list of ways things stink. So I began to acquire the skill of saying things in a more tactful manner. But the other day I had this unfiltered thought that sounds a lot like the older brother. Here's the thought: Sometimes serving God seems boring.

I know I shouldn't feel this way, but I do. I'm not sure if this is from the devil or from my own brain, but it just feels tiresome. At times, serving God can feel to me much the same as a job that is unsatisfying and routine and stinky—like cleaning the stalls after the horses leave the barn. When this feeling persists, I can get lost in the picture of drudgery, and I am deceived into believing that this is just how life is and I might as well get used to it.

I empathize with the older brother, because even though he's lost, he doesn't mean to be. He really thinks he's doing the right thing. By looking at his résumé, I notice that he's serving at his father's house and apparently in the family business. He's working hard—at least by his own account—and is likely doing his job to the best of his ability. He would have been courted by Democrats and Republicans both as an example of "the working man." Jesus tells us that when the elder brother found out about the party for his wild and lazy younger brother, "He answered his father, 'Listen! All these years I've worked like a slave for you. I've never disobeyed a command of yours'" (Luke 15:29, ISV). This is the cry of injustice. And as I read this, I sense that deep down I tend to follow his line of thinking more than I would like to admit. I really do long for a world where people are rewarded for good behavior and punished for foolishness, where faithfulness and hard work really do help us get all we could ever want out of life.

I believe that the attitude of the elder brother is extremely common in most churches. Since I have been a behind-the-scenes part of church my entire life, I have some room to speak here. Here's the deal: churches that have been well-established for a number of years tend to attract those with a stable faith and a desire for predictability and order. Along with their bodies, most of these people bring their beliefs in a "cause and effect" kind of God, the kind of God who gives a formula for success, where when I do "A" combined with "B" I will always get "C."

These are people who mainly work hard and pay their taxes and may even tithe. They don't like slackers, and they really want the hardest-working people to get the most benefits out of life. People like me, in all honesty, mostly want a God who operates primarily by formula and can be controlled by good behavior.

In other words, I think we're partial to a God who is tame. The idea of a God who doesn't behave the same way every time is frankly a little dangerous to most people. That's the troubling part of the prodigal story for me. This story shows us a side of the Father that doesn't agree with my presuppositions about reward and punishment. This story shows me a Father who is unpredictable and a little crazy with His resources. This story makes me uncomfortable.

It is not safe.

I love to be safe, don't you? I'm a little like a vulture on the side of the road that doesn't venture out in the middle for fear of getting hit. But even though I like to be safe, I also love to go to the zoo. At the zoo I get to exercise, get outside, and even tap the glass at the monkey cage if I want to. I'm always amazed at the variety of life our God has given us to enjoy. For me, a trip to the zoo is a spiritual experience of worship and thanksgiving. But when I go to the zoo, I'm also thankful for a few things—namely the bars and fences and shatterproof glass. These are the happy barriers that separate me from lions and tigers and bears. They allow me to view any of the caged beasts while also providing me the safety of knowing that I will in no way become a meal. I prefer a zoo with boundaries.

In a similar way, a tame God—a God who stays within the lines of one's imagination and never behaves outside of expectations—is equally preferable to our modern sensibilities. But God is not safe, and He is definitely not an I-get-what-I-deserve kind of God. Over and over, the Bible points out that our God is a God of mercy, and mercy is when I don't get what I deserve. The prodigal story points out what a difficult idea mercy is to those who prefer a tame God who stays safely in the boundaries of a behavior-driven rewards system.

I believe Jesus was pointing us to the fact that hard work is not the goal of life, although hard work is always a key virtue in life. Working hard for a monetary or moral reward will never be enough to fulfill a human soul. The Scriptures repeatedly scream to us that love is the ultimate gift and the ultimate goal of life. Using myself as an example, I know that when I love other people, for their benefit, I am always satisfied. I never get bored when I really love others with no agenda attached. Love is fun. Loving other people carries within itself the biggest reward. And love is the point of life on this earth—not hard work, not achievement, or accomplishment. All of those are a part of life, but not the point of life. The point of life is love.

Jesus affirmed this one day in a teaching moment when He was grilled by the religious elite.

> One of them, an expert in the law, tested him with this question: "Teacher, which is the greatest commandment in the Law?" Jesus replied: 'Love the Lord your God with all your heart and with all your soul and with all your mind.' This is the first and greatest commandment. And the second is like it: Love your neighbor as yourself. All the Law and the Prophets hang on these two commandments,'" (*Matthew 22:35-40*).

It sure seems that Jesus was putting a premium on the idea of love.

The older brother worked hard and put forth a record of obedience that he was proud enough to declare to his father as something worthy of consideration. But he missed the point; he didn't love.

So let's change the prodigal story, and let's assume the older brother understands that the point of life is love and that he should love his brother as he loves himself. And since I'm writing this, I get to tell how it would have gone. If the older brother had understood the point of life, he would have been the one running to get the fattened calf. The father's celebration would have become his celebration as well. Instead of being grumpy, he would have been accommodating. Instead of listing his work accomplishments, he would have been gathering wood and lighting a fire for the feast. He would have had a smile and a faster heart rate. His work would not have been a drudgery or boring or routine. His work would have been flowing from love, and that love would have provided joy and a party-hearty attitude. That's a story that God can tell through anyone who will make the choice to love His lost children as much as He does.

Honestly, I wish my spiritual journey was marked more often by love—pure, selfless love. And I know that's the missing element in my life when I think that serving God is getting a little tiresome and uneventful. It's the missing motivation when I have allowed another attitude to dominate my life that is anti-love and anti-Christ. My other attitude doesn't wear horns or have the number 666 in it. It simply goes by the benign name of "selfishness." Selfishness sounds a bit juvenile but certainly not sinister—don't you agree? But I'm seeing more and more that this little word has caused just about every relational and emotional malady there ever was, including elder brother-itis. Here are a few examples.

A man and woman get divorced. And what was the root cause? It's always selfishness. A good employee gets overlooked for a promotion or raise and becomes permanently angry and unproductive. Another holds a grudge and refuses to forgive his or her parents, which leads to a life of misery and self-destruction. Why? You already know why: selfishness.

A teenage child decides to disobey his or her parents and picks up friends while driving under the influence of alcohol. An accident happens and people get hurt, all because somebody wanted to feel a buzz and forsake the consequences. Underneath that first choice to drink was basic, self-centered, self-love. I could go on and on, and so could you. If you examine your attitudes and actions right now and look to see where you are having the biggest problems, I am willing to bet that one hundred percent of it is being caused by your own selfishness.

Even if someone else is wronging you and hurting you deeply, your reaction is going to be out of love or out of selfishness, and your reaction will be determining your own peace of mind. More important, it will determine your connection to your Father God.

Let me honestly say that sometimes serving our Father God is tiresome. But it's tiresome only when my service to the Father is really veiled self-service because of the goodies He will give me if I am a good boy. It's boring when I live by merit instead of mercy and grace. However, serving the Father is never tiresome or boring when I'm doing it out of love for Him and solely for the sake of others.

Do you see how the Father is pleading with you right now, just as the earthly father pleaded with the older son? God is offering a feast for you today. The feast is always available. The feast He is offering is the choice to love. To love is to feast! So today see the world as your smorgasbord, and seek out anyone with skin on and dive in and show him or her love. By doing this, you will be feeding your soul on the finest of foods, and you will in turn feed this broken world what it most desperately needs. The Beatles had it right on one account—all you need is love.

Can You Relate?

Read through the following questions and record your thoughts and reactions.

1. Are you more like the first or second vulture? What has hesitation kept you from experiencing? In what situations are you willing to go for it, and in which situations do you hesitate?

_____

_____

_____

_____

_____

_____

_____

_____

_____

_____

_____

_____

_____

2. What is God pleading with you to do? Do you accept all His blessings or hang back if things don't go exactly the way you expected?

_____

_____

_____

_____

_____

_____

_____

_____

_____

_____

_____

_____

_____

_____

_____

_____

_____

_____

_____

_____

3. Jesus told His followers to be like children in Matthew
   18:3. "Kids Say the Darndest Things" was a popular
   television show that proved that one thing people admire
   about children is their honesty. Do you agree that honesty can be a dangerous thing? In what situations? How
   can a Christian balance both the positives and negatives
   of being honest?

   _____

   _____

   _____

   _____

   _____

   _____

   _____

   _____

   _____

   _____

   _____

   _____

   _____

   _____

4. Does your church simply attract more believers? Would a non-believer or new Christian fit in at your church? Have you ever looked down on someone who didn't act in the expected ways?

_____

_____

_____

_____

_____

_____

_____

_____

_____

_____

_____

_____

_____

_____

_____

_____

_____

_____

_____

5. Think of the greatest moments in your life. How many of them were planned? How many of them happened exactly as they were planned? Would you look back on those moments as just as great if nothing about them was spontaneous or different from your expectations? How do you see God? Is He a God of cause and effect, or is He just as unpredictable as the greatest moments of your life?

_____

_____

_____

_____

_____

_____

_____

_____

_____

_____

_____

_____

_____

_____

_____

6. Who would you put on the list of the most important people in your life? Did God make the list? How do you show these people they are important? Why do you do things for them? Is serving God an item on your checklist or something you do out of love?

_____

_____

_____

_____

_____

_____

_____

_____

_____

_____

_____

_____

_____

_____

_____

_____

_____

SIX

THE THREE TREES

Look! All these years I've been slaving
for you and never disobeyed your orders.

—Luke 15:29

My first official job that didn't involve mowing lawns was when I was fifteen and working at America's favorite flame-broiled hangout, Burger King. I learned two important lessons for life while working there.

First, flame-broiling truly is the best way to cook a burger. There is just no substitute for the special taste of charred flesh that cannot be duplicated on a flameless hot griddle. The debate is over.

The second message is a little saying that management, or "the man," as we knew them, came up with. The man would say to fresh-eyed recruits like me, "Boy, if you've got time to lean, you've got time to clean."

The first time I heard it, I was looking for said boy and sheepishly learned that I was that boy, so I picked up the nearest rag. You know—the rag. It's the same rag that cleans up everything at restaurants, including the table you aren't supposed to put your elbows on. The rag was stiff with an untraceable and unknowable foreign substance, so I got it wet with a measured amount of the universal solvent (H_2O), and started cleaning.

The man didn't say how to clean—he just said clean, so I did what generations have done before and since. I smeared at stuff until it disappeared. Everybody was pleased that the tables looked clean and I looked busy. It was in that moment that I learned an important lesson about working. It can pay to look busy, even if what you're doing doesn't matter. In fact, this very second as you read this, there are likely millions of people sitting at desks, walking with serious purpose in restaurants, or intently staring at computer screens, getting paid to do nothing other than appear extremely busy.

In my eleven-year corporate career, I learned that busy people are generally regarded as the hard workers in big companies, whether or not the work that is being done is very productive in the long run. Obviously, sometimes these busy people are the real producers—but not always. Sometimes the smart and productive people—who don't want to fake it and just look the part—can appear lazy and unmotivated at tasks that don't offer a challenge or require much real effort. It takes a good manager to know the difference between a person who is producing good results and a person who is just frantically buzzing about. But over time I have noticed, as my mom once told me, "The cream always rises to the top." (At Starbucks they save us from observing this settling action and just offer the whipped cream on top, as it should be.)

This adage about cream is true in business, and it is true in my own spiritual journey as well. Like the older brother, I can sometimes equate spiritual growth with spiritual busy-ness. And if you have followed Jesus for any length of time, you probably share this same blind spot.

As I write this, I am sitting on my back porch in my home in Lakeland, Florida, on a dry October day. I say dry, because in Lakeland there are two kinds of weather to enjoy: dry or humid. When it's dry, it's usually because a north wind is blowing and there are no clouds in the sky. People move to this part of the world because of these dry days that generally occur from December to March in this part of the humid subtropical zone. But for most months, the dampness is pretty stifling, which makes outdoor writing more difficult. So I'm really enjoying this weather while it's here.

Lakeland is a beautiful, medium-sized city stuck right in the middle between Orlando and Tampa on the I-4 corridor in central Florida. Central Florida is historically known for three things as far as industry goes: cattle, phosphate, and citrus. And citrus trees love three things that we have here in abundance. They thrive because of the moist climate, the mild winters, and the fast-draining, sandy soil. Just over the fence in my backyard are three tangerine trees growing on an undeveloped piece of land that also includes raccoons, native palm trees, live oaks with heavy doses of dangling Spanish moss, and squirrels that really bother me. Squirrels have always bothered me as far back as I remember. I used to love to chase them as a child, and they were always able to evade me as they hid on the backside of every trunk as they climbed. I never did catch one—a fact I'm very happy about today as I still have all ten fingers intact. Squirrels just have an arrogant way about them, don't you think?

So I was looking at these three tangerine trees last February over the back fence, and I noticed that since nobody was tending these trees, there were a whole bunch of vines that were growing up into the canopy. All three trees had ripened tangerines, but nowhere near the numbers or size they should have been producing. The vines were choking the life from each tree. So as a tree lover, I set out to do my part. The fact that these trees could produce more real food in the future compelled me to get to work. I like trees that make food. I climbed the fence armed with this love for nature, a small saw, pruning clippers, and some leather gloves.

Before I go further, let me say that from thirty yards away—the distance from my back porch seat to the trees—all three trees appeared to be about the same canopy size and trunk diameter and had the same shape, fullness, and greenery. They looked like healthy, twenty-five-foot trees with a little extra alien vine growth. Tree one had the healthiest-looking leaves, in that they were the deepest green but had the smallest fruit. So I started there, and it took about twenty minutes of cutting and yanking. The most common vine I found was the Virginia Creeper, which adds little foot-like roots to the trunk as it twists vertically toward the light. I would clip the base of the vine nearest the ground and use my body weight to pull the vines out and wind them up. I looked back and felt pleased at my work. One down, two to go.

The second tree was different. It had the same vine problem—in fact, even more. But it was also losing light because of an oak that was producing too much shade. The funny thing to me was that this tree still had better tangerines than the first, even with the lack of light and the additional vines. Two down, one to go.

The last tree was a little more complex. It had looked very healthy from my porch, but it was anything but. As I began cutting at the vines, I noticed a difference. These vines were thicker and tougher to cut and pull. On some vines I had to pull with my entire body weight like Tarzan, but many wouldn't come out. There were three different species of vine that I was unfamiliar with in this tree as well. But the most difficult was one that expanded at the top; I've since learned it is called "skunk vine." At the ground, skunk vine is thin and green, but at the top of the tree, where the light is best, this crazy vine explodes with a very top-heavy, fireworks-like design. It is known to kill trees just from the sheer weight it adds to each branch. To top it off, its leaf shape and color closely match the host tree. In other words, from a distance this skunk vine, which was killing its host, made the tree appear healthier than it really was. The danger in this kind of vine is the lie it's telling.

After working for two hours, I finally finished with the third tree. And as I looked at it without vines, I was really stunned. Tree number three looked like a skeleton of its former self. At least half of the greenery was now gone. Old limbs that were dead or diseased I cut out. They had simply provided a path for these lying vines that masked the deterioration happening underneath. I was black with dirt and grime and sweat. Did I mention that I did this work in the humid season? My friend Rick says if you want to know the climate in Lakeland most of the time, just stick your finger in your mouth. And that's pretty-much how it felt outside that day. But on the inside I had a feeling of satisfaction, because I knew that in the long run all three trees had at least the potential for greater health.

When I sat down with a couple of bottles of water next to me, God decided to pay me a visit. He seemed to speak to me and tell me, "Brett, that's what you do. That's what I created you to do for other people, not just trees. You help people by showing them how to become healthy by first showing them the lies they're believing." In effect, I felt as if God were defining my personal ministry that day as weed-puller. And I was okay with that, because it seems to fit.

As I said before, the danger with the vines on this last tree was the lie that it was telling. This tree spoke to the world through greenery, and most observers assumed health on first glance. The older son in the prodigal parable had the same problem. He pointed his father back to his hard work as evidence of his right standing in the family. He was able to look in the mirror and assume his place in the family based on activity instead of love.

Theologians agree that Jesus had the Pharisee group in mind when telling this story. The Pharisees, like the older brother, worked hard at their faith. They were clearly the most strident of the Jewish men, and they wanted everyone to know about it. Their faith was a very public piety—another fact that Jesus would speak to in various places during the Sermon on the Mount in Matthew 5-7. Pharisees took pride in their pain, but they did what many do today—they missed the point of serving their Heavenly Father.

When the older son was confronted by his father's mercy, he pointed to his record of works. But the terse reply also shows that the heart of the older brother was cold against both the father and his brother. He served slavishly but didn't love extravagantly. And his problem is still a problem in churches today. Honestly, it's still my problem. I'm the older brother in the story. I've been in the religious system all my life. I get that, so I know to beware of this tendency. But I still have problems identifying this same stinking attitude when it creeps into my head and explodes from idea into behavior. I forget that the point of life is found by loving God and by loving His kids. I forget that the point of my life is not how many people attend my church. I forget that the point of my life is not how many books I write or how many sermons I preach or how many hours I spend on my knees for God. I forget that God is not impressed by scripture memorization or my small-group attendance. I have a tendency to let religious activity be a substitute for real love. And from what I've observed, this is a pretty widespread problem among my Christian tribe.

It's always easy to forget the basics in any endeavor. Every time I golf I forget to look at the ball. I have to remind myself, *Brett, keep your eye on the ball.* The game doesn't change from shot to shot, but my ability to focus does. Even Tiger Woods loses his golf swing from time to time. When I carry on a conversation while driving my car, I have a propensity to weave in my lane. I talk with my hands, I guess, and when I do, I have that voice in my head saying, *Keep your eyes on the road.* Or maybe it's an echo of the voice of the one in the passenger seat. Sometimes it's hard to tell with voices. Focus can be hard.

The honest thing I want to communicate to you is simply this: even the best Christians struggle with focus from time to time. It doesn't necessarily have anything to do with the devil or our sinful nature or anything like that. It happens because in our busy world, with hyperactive schedules and appetites driving people from hither to yon, it is just plain easy to forget what is truly most important in life. Forgetfulness is human.

So let's go back to the tangerine trees. How does a person judge when a tangerine tree is good? Simple—it bears fruit. The key thing I learned is that I can't judge a tangerine tree by its leaves. And the same is true in my spiritual journey. I can't really judge my own spiritual journey based on a set of external evidence—or works, as the older brother was prone to do. I have to stop and search for the kind of fruit that you can't see on a calendar or observe on a spreadsheet. Spiritual fruit, like love, joy, peace, patience, kindness, goodness, gentleness, faithfulness, and self-control, is harder to detect. In fact, it's much easier to fill a calendar with spiritual activities than it is to honestly produce that kind of fruit.

Discerning real life and soul growth is impossible without self-examination. And it's a real possibility in our culture to let religious activity destroy the life that God intended for us to have. Here's the real problem: the Pharisee sect in Jesus' day was living proof that spiritual activity can become an idol in and of itself. I believe this idol may be a major factor that explains the lack of numerical growth and cultural impact of the North American Church. Self-sufficiency always crowds God out of first place. Jeremiah spoke for God one day and issued these words to people like us:

> "Has any nation ever traded its gods for new ones, even though they are not gods at all? Yet my people have exchanged their glorious Gods for worthless idols! The heavens are shocked at such a thing and shrink back in horror and dismay," says the LORD. "For my people have done two evil things: They have abandoned me—the fountain of living water. And they have dug for themselves cracked cisterns that can hold no water at all!" *(Jeremiah 2:11-13, NLT)*

Notice what has happened. They traded gods. Instead of a fountain of purity and life and protection, they chose their own path, a way of life that literally couldn't hold water. I think Jeremiah may look at today's churches and speak the same word.

Have churches forsaken God and embraced familiar programming, even if that programming isn't producing fruit? Have they embraced cracked human methods that may have worked for others in the past but are not driven by God today? The more I read, the more I see that some churches are embracing the very separatist attitudes that the Pharisees maintained—the same cracked thinking that Jesus vehemently opposed that leads to spiritual death while giving the appearance of life.

I read this scripture and pray, *God, I want to stay by the fountain. I don't want to do things for you in my strength that you*

*don't enjoy or desire. I don't want to do things for you—I want to
do things with you!*

I want to end this chapter by giving a few alternatives
to simply maintaining a spiritually busy life. If you are in-
clined to pray the same prayer that I just prayed, I want you
to read these words from the apostle Paul to have the tem-
plate of what a real fruitful life with God looks like:

> And this is my prayer: that your love may abound
> more and more in knowledge and depth of insight, so
> that you may be able to discern what is best and may
> be pure and blameless until the day of Christ, filled
> with the fruit of righteousness that comes through Je-
> sus Christ—to the glory and praise of God. *(Philippians
> 1:9-11)*

Three things in those verses are given as proof of
spiritual vitality and growth. The first sign of true spiritual
growth is that your love for other people is growing. Verse 9
begins, "And this is my prayer: that your love may abound."
The kind of love spoken of here is not sentimental. In fact,
this kind of love is well thought out and not driven by im-
pulse or feeling. And it is the kind of love that overflows and
flourishes. So as you read this verse, ask yourself a revealing
question: Is my love for other people really growing, or is it
shrinking?

This kind of love is a choice rather than a feeling. Con-
tinuing with verse 9, we read, "that your love may abound
more and more in knowledge." In other words, a growing
Christian is learning what love is and what love isn't.

When counseling married couples, I have found that many spouses want to give the other party what they want to give them, because it's what they want in return. And many times in doing this, they fail to give what the other party really wants. In other words, they try to love, but they don't have love combined with knowledge. Love combined and abounding with knowledge knows what to do at the right time and does it. Mindy and I have been married nearly twenty-five years. There are certain things I know now that I didn't know when we got married. And I'm really trying to apply what I know, because when I do this, combine love with knowledge, it's a good day to be me.

Verse 9 concludes by adding, "that your love may abound more and more in knowledge and depth of insight." It's one thing to learn what it means to love, but it's another thing to learn better how to love. When your loving adds depth of insight, you become the person who knows what to do and when to do it. I've met many young men who want to impress their young ladies. They launch the big guns all at once and don't know what to do next. As you begin to bear fruit in life, you become a person others check with before making big decisions. A growing, fruitful Christian is in high demand in this world. The fruit is so attractive when the fruit is abounding love.

The second sign of true spiritual growth is a growing understanding of God's will. Paul continues, "So that you may be able to discern what is best and may be pure and blameless until the day of Christ" (Philippians 1:10). The best things are "God things." The older son in the prodigal story, like many today, forgot what his father was really like. He made a horrible assumption when he said to his father, "You never gave me even a young goat so I could celebrate with my friends" (Luke 15:29). He assumed the worst about his father, so he never even asked for a party. He didn't understand his father's willingness and generosity. "'My son,' the father said, 'you are always with me, and everything I have is yours,'" (Luke 15:31).

A person who discerns what is best is able to understand his or her place in God's family, because he or she understands His heart. As a result, the person does his or her best to live a life of sincerity and honesty before Him, for the good of others. In fact, the word in Philippians 1:10 that's translated "pure" can also be translated "sincere." Purity and sincerity are always qualities that add value to other people. A pure mountain stream gives life to others just as a sincerely paid compliment brings hope to the one receiving it. Conversely, a polluted, stagnant well, or flattery that is not based in truth, can do a great deal of harm. The positive picture is one of a growing Christian full of God's abounding love.

The third evidence of true spiritual growth is the growth of your impact on this world. Paul concludes his thought by praying, "That you may be . . . filled with the fruit of righteousness that comes through Jesus Christ—to the glory and praise of God" (Philippians 1:10-11). Paul's hope and prayer was for Christian people to become more like Jesus Christ, to be filled with righteousness, and in so doing they would bring glory and praise to God. Over the course of my life I have been around a whole bunch of pastors. I have four pastors in my immediate family and many more in the extended tree. I can tell you for certain that this prayer can be answered. I have watched my family produce a tremendous amount of spiritual fruit in lives that were changed. And when I allow God's love and His life to flow through me, I am certain to produce a life that is needed and attractive to a world that is in real need of real hope. The neat thing is that you don't have to get old to see this happen. In my church I am currently watching two young teen girls, Emily and Allison, produce lives filled with righteousness, thereby bringing glory to God.

Emily Osley was attending a Christian summer camp with a group from our church here in Florida when she was confronted by a video showing the global problem of clean water, specifically the horrible conditions facing the people of Zambia. An organization called Active Water was soliciting assistance through the video, and Emily was moved to action. She talked about it with her friend, Allison Beatty, and they decided to do what they could do to raise money. They decided on sewing tiny birds, about the size of Christmas ornaments, and making them available to friends and family for the cost of five dollars each. All the proceeds would go to Active Water, and their goal was to raise five hundred dollars. Youth Pastor Brooklyn Lindsey got involved and got them set up on Facebook to help with marketing. One Sunday I allowed them to share their burden with our congregation. Since then, in only two months of active marketing, they have raised over four thousand dollars, and now the goal is ten thousand dollars. The Lakeland *Ledger* even highlighted their story with a sectional front-page story.[3]

This kind of miracle is real fruit of righteousness, not just a religious display.

So what about you today? Is there any evidence in your life that you are growing in love for others? Is God's will becoming clearer and clearer to you? Are you really producing fruit of righteousness that's bringing glory to God? If the answers are yes to all three, then praise God. But if not, what should you do?

As you read this, I want you to stop and ask God to identify the real problem. For the tangerine trees, the problems weren't obvious at first. It took some work to expose the issues. If you pray and ask God for insight here, He will give it to you. But He won't give it all to you at once. He will just ask you to be obedient to do that next one thing. As I once heard Dallas Willard say, "If you want to grow in your Christian journey, simply do the next right thing that you come to."

If you pray for God to help you identify your real problems—or weeds—in life, then get busy and pull the weeds and expose the damage. Christians should be on the lookout for lies that sneak in like creepy vines. Vines don't move quickly like a rabbit—they move at a snail's pace. In the same way, most bad behavior is driven by subtle lies accepted over time as normal. Pulling the weeds, the vines of sin, out of your life will require honesty and Holy-Spirit-inspired effort. After you've done that, simply let the light shine and heal what was broken so that it can bear more fruit.

Jesus once encouraged His small band of followers with a fruitful analogy like this:

> I am the true vine, and my Father is the gardener. He cuts off every branch in me that bears no fruit, while every branch that does bear fruit he prunes so that it will be even more fruitful. Remain in me, as I also remain in you. No branch can bear fruit by itself; it must remain in the vine. Neither can you bear fruit unless you remain in me. I am the vine; you are the branches. If you remain in me and I in you, you will bear much fruit; apart from me you can do nothing. *(John 15:1-5)*

My prayer for you is that you will allow God to tear the bad stuff out of your life, with your full knowledge and co-operation. By doing this, you will bear much fruit and bring glory to our generous and loving Father, who has a plan for you that also includes chasing down those lost and wayward brothers and sisters before they get so lost in the first place.

So he got up and went to his father. But while he was still a long way off, his father saw him and was filled with compassion for him; he ran to his son, threw his arms around him and kissed him (Luke 15:20).

Can You Relate?

Read through the following questions and record your thoughts and reactions.

1. How would a good manager classify your spiritual life? Are you actually busy, or do you simply appear busy? Are there specific areas you always seem to be busy in and others where you always only appear busy?

_____

_____

_____

_____

_____

_____

_____

_____

_____

_____

_____

_____

_____

_____

_____

_____

2. Which of the three trees is your spiritual life most like? Are you tree number one, whose spiritual life outwardly looks healthy and busy, with only some minor, socially accepted vines but whose fruit is not as good as it could be? Are you tree two, a believer who has some unavoidable disadvantage, like the lack of sunlight, but who is making the best of the situation? Or are you tree three, who seems to be the best but whose spiritual life is bare, full of dead, diseased branches mixed with vines pretending to be branches?

_____

_____

_____

_____

_____

_____

_____

_____

_____

_____

_____

_____

_____

3. Just as there are methods for focusing on everyday tasks, there are methods of keeping yourself focused on God and what is important in life. Whether it's a reminder in your phone to do devotions or a sticky note on the mirror with an important verse, how do you keep yourself focused on God? How could you improve on the ways you already have in place?

_____

_____

_____

_____

_____

_____

_____

_____

_____

_____

_____

_____

_____

_____

_____

_____

4. Have you ever heard someone say he or she got divorced because he or she no longer loved his or her spouse? What those people fail to realize is that love is not an emotion—it is a choice. Are you choosing to love God every day? In what new ways could you actively decide to love God?

_____

_____

_____

_____

_____

_____

_____

_____

_____

_____

_____

_____

_____

_____

_____

_____

_____

_____

5. A sign of true love is complete trust in the other person. Do you trust God to prune whatever He sees fit in your life? What areas do you hold close to yourself, and which areas do you willingly give to Him?

_____

_____

_____

_____

_____

_____

_____

_____

_____

_____

_____

_____

_____

_____

_____

_____

_____

_____

_____

6. Merriam-Webster defines righteousness as "acting in accordance with divine or moral law; morally right or justifiable." What does being righteous mean to you? How can you be an example of righteousness to others?

_____

_____

_____

_____

_____

_____

_____

_____

_____

_____

_____

_____

_____

_____

_____

_____

_____

_____

SECTION THREE

The Father

SEVEN

THE WIZ

*The L*ORD *redeems his servants; no one*
will be condemned who takes refuge in him.

—Psalm 34:22

Not long ago I watched a movie that I had wanted to see for years but had never made the time. The movie is called *The Wiz*, starring a younger Diana Ross and Michael Jackson. *The Wiz* is a seventies urban remake of the classic *The Wizard of Oz*, complete with funky wardrobe, dance, and music. In fact, it was the kind of music that made white folks get perms and wear Afros. The trailer and movie poster were intriguing, so when I finally got a chance to see it, my hopes were pretty high.

Sadly, my expectations far exceeded reality. To be honest, I couldn't bring myself to stay interested in the movie for five minutes on the small screen in my living room without channel surfing. I did reengage one time when they sang "Ease On Down the Road," but that was about it. The rest of the time I flipped back and forth between the two Big S's in my life, SpongeBob SquarePants and SportsCenter. *The Wiz* was a first-class flop and didn't match the hype, at least in my mind.

Everyone has experienced the crash that comes when certain unanticipated realities of life materialize and bear no resemblance to the preconceived fantasy of how things could or should be. For instance, I know people who had one view of married life in mind, only to learn on their honeymoon how things would be quite different. The same can be said of most first-time parents living through that seemingly endless first year with their first child. Chicago Cubs fans feel this every year. Forethought and reality rarely coincide. But the saddest instance for me as a pastor is when people have a warped impression of our Heavenly father.

Many Christians and non-Christians unwittingly believe that God is a lot like the wizard of Oz. Though they may not vocalize it that way, they live the kind of life that reflects this kind of faith. For example, a person may believe the Father, like the wizard, lives behind a curtain, or "in Heaven," wherever that may be. They believe that He is magical and mystical and may indeed have all the answers— but is likely a little scatterbrained, since the world is so big and He has so much to look after. Since He loves humans, He's therefore quite harmless. They may even sometimes conceive that He can be found only after a great search that is filled with good deeds, the correct direction, and proper attire, of course.

In his book *Your God Is Too Small*, author J. B. Phillips teaches that many Christians and non-Christians alike have similar misconceptions of God. He believes that these flawed pictures of God keep people from true worship. He states,

> Many men and women today are living, often with inner dissatisfaction, without any faith in God at all. This is not because they are particularly wicked or selfish . . . but because they have not found with their adult minds a God big enough to "account for" life, big enough to "fit in with" the new scientific age, big enough to command their highest admiration and respect, and consequently their willing cooperation.[1]

But the picture of our Heavenly Father in the prodigal parable is nothing like that of *The Wiz*, or what Phillips would call the "Grand Old Man" view of God. Where the old and out-of-touch Wiz is detached and hard to find, the Father appears to be engaged and watching out. Where the Wiz requires certain hoops be jumped through prior to an award, the Father offers the reward without behavioral strings attached. Where the Wiz waits for people to come to him, the Father runs to meet those searching for life's answers. While the Wiz has illusory power given to him by those who believe he can do something—when he can't— the Father actually has real power to restore and rebuild. In *The Wizard of Oz*, the saddest moment in the film comes when the powerless wizard, who planned to get Dorothy back to Kansas, accidentally flies away in his balloon, leaving Dorothy again to fend for herself, stuck in Oz. The Father is no "fly-away" wizard. In fact, I want to take a look back in the Book of Psalms at one of my all-time favorite songs about God to get a clearer picture of what our Heavenly Father is really like and how we can respond to His goodness. He is a God of endless hope. Since this psalm— or song—was written as a whole, I want to leave it that way and then go back and go deeper.

I will extol the LORD at all times; his praise will always be on my lips. My soul will boast in the LORD; let the afflicted hear and rejoice. Glorify the LORD with me; let us exalt his name together. I sought the LORD, and he answered me; he delivered me from all my fears.

Those who look to him are radiant; their faces are never covered with shame. This poor man called, and the LORD heard him; he saved him out of all his troubles. The angel of the LORD encamps around those who fear him, and he delivers them. Taste and see that the LORD is good; blessed is the man who takes refuge in him. Fear the LORD, you his saints, for those who fear him lack nothing. The lions may grow weak and hungry, but those who seek the LORD lack no good thing. Come, my children, listen to me; I will teach you the fear of the LORD. Whoever of you loves life and desires to see many good days, keep your tongue from evil and your lips from speaking lies. Turn from evil and do good; seek peace and pursue it. The eyes of the LORD are on the righteous and his ears are attentive to their cry; the face of the LORD is against those who do evil, to cut off the memory of them from the earth. The righteous cry out, and the LORD hears them; he delivers them from all their troubles. The LORD is close to the brokenhearted and saves those who are crushed in spirit. A righteous man may have many troubles, but the LORD delivers him from them all; he protects all his bones, not one of them will be broken. Evil will slay the wicked; the foes of the righteous will be condemned. The LORD redeems his servants; no one will be condemned who takes refuge in him. *(Psalm 34:1-22)*

Isn't that a beautiful picture of how the Lord deals with us in our reality? Our Heavenly Father, as revealed here and in the prodigal parable, is a God of hope. In fact, in this song I see five ways that Father God brings me hope.

First, He takes my calls. Verse 4 says "I sought the LORD, and he answered me." This is what fathers do—though in my case it's not always the moment my kids ask me for something. If they make a request for me to play dominoes with them, for instance, in the middle of an Oklahoma football game, that request may be ignored in the short term. But if their request is truly urgent, they always get an answer. The fact that the God of the universe is available the moment I call for Him is truly amazing. I don't have that kind of access to my mayor, my governor, my president, or even my hair stylist. In fact, it's hard to get anybody to take my calls, especially friends under thirty. When I grew up, there was a race to answer the phone when it rang. If someone valued my time and liked me enough to call me, the thinking went, I should be honored to answer that call. The ringer had the power. But then caller ID happened and choice followed, and now it's really hard to get young people who have grown up without honoring the power of the ring to take my calls—maybe because they don't always feel as if they have the time or inclination to talk.

With God, the ringer still has the power. If we call, He answers. But His answers are not always yes, and we don't always know the moment our request is fully answered. And just as when my kids ask me for candy before dinner, sometimes our requests to God are met with a no. If fact, I heard an old preacher say that God gives us four answers when we call out to him. He can say, "Yes," "No," "Slow," or "Grow." The "Yes" is my favorite, but I've learned to appreciate His "No" as well. Garth Brooks recorded a hit song that captures the value of God's "No" titled "Unanswered Prayers." It tells a story about a fellow and his wife who run into his old flame. He had prayed for God to make the old flame take him back when he was in high school, but God's answer had been "No." When he ran into her years later, he saw that God's wisdom in saying no had saved him a lot of grief.

Thankfully, sometimes God says, "No." At other times God will answer, but His answer is "Slow," or in other words, "Wait." Some of the things we think we need and ask for now are really meant for later.

My youngest daughter, Hope, is the one in our family who has the hardest time waiting. If we drive for more than twenty minutes, she begins the steady barrage of "Are we there yet?" "How long is it going to be?" "When are we going to be there?" She just doesn't like the idea that she has to wait. But in God's economy, timing is a big deal. When He makes us wait, we rarely know the entire reason for the wait and likely never will this side of eternity, but after following Him for many years, I know that though He may make me wait, He is never late!

His answer to a request may also be "Grow." This is the answer I will never understand except in the rearview mirror of life. One of the ways I pray best is through a daily prayer journal. I write it so I have a record of God's activity in my life; otherwise I forget. Then in my journal I can look back at my requests and see the ones where God didn't answer the way I wanted. In fact, it seems as if in those times He is silent. But these are times that God invites me to continue seeking for Him with a little more effort. Here in central Florida things grow like crazy. In fact, too many things grow. Weeds here can get to the size of small trees in no time. And as I mentioned earlier, many vines here grow along the ground and find tree trunks to climb. You can't miss their tendency to reach for the light. Vines don't get in a hurry; they just keep reaching up. When God tells me to wait and grow, it's not time to quit—it's just time to keep pressing toward the light.

The second way God gives me hope is that He calms my fears. Verse 4 says, "He delivered me from all my fears." I've heard it said that fear is faith in reverse; and we live in a world that can be dominated by fear. Nearly every local and national cable news channel gives an easy-to-follow, blow-by-blow eyewitness account of mortal dangers both at home and abroad. Local newspapers are filled with stories of crime and police drama, teenage suicide, and drug addiction. If a person isn't careful, fear can quickly become the dominant vibe. Psychologists have even come up with a new term to describe a life dealing with the palpable, physical onslaught of fear. They call these momentary battles "panic attacks." Anyone who has ever struggled with these can tell you that fear, no matter the source, feels like being on a freight train that is running out of control. But our Heavenly Father calms my fears as I continue to learn to give them to Him.

Third, my Father takes away my shame. "Those who look to him are radiant; their faces are never covered with shame" (Psalm 34:5). Guilt and shame are the toxic twins that keep people locked up in the failures of the past. I remember the first time I told a lie to my mom. I think I was around four years old, and it happened in my basement. Mom came down and asked me if I had done something. I don't remember what it was I was trying to hide, but I lied and said that I hadn't. I do remember that my stomach turned somersaults. I felt bad and learned firsthand what shame does on the inside of a person.

As adults, dealing with shame is a much bigger deal, especially as the size of the consequences grows. For instance, telling a lie to Mom may land a person in hot water for a moment, but the consequences of cheating on a spouse, having an abortion, or committing a crime carry a lot more public baggage. And when other people get to see the dirty laundry, it can seem as if the shame will go on forever. Shame separates friends, and it separates people from their Heavenly Father. Remember what Adam did after he sinned? He hid from God, and then he made the first pair of Speedos. Shame reduces us to hiding out and covering up, but this psalm promises that God takes away our shame.

Fourth, He shields me from bigger trouble.

> This poor man called, and the LORD heard him; he saved him out of all his troubles. The angel of the LORD encamps around those who fear him, and he *delivers* them. *(Psalm 34:6-7, emphasis added)*

The Lord hears, saves, encamps around, and delivers. And all the poor man had to do was call.

I love the picture that I saw as a child that portrayed a big man holding the earth in his hands. The big man was supposed to be the Father, and it helped me visualize the scale of His greatness to a certain degree. I know He's even bigger than that scaled-down version, but for my sake, it helps me see His size and then imagine His power. When I pray, theologically I know God is present, because His Spirit lives in me, but I also like to picture that big God leaning His ear toward my present location. Seeing God as big gives me more faith so that no matter what I'm dealing with, I remember that God is bigger, that He still saves me, encamps around me, and delivers me.

Fifth, He comforts my broken heart. This promises a softer dimension of God's greatness: "The LORD is close to the brokenhearted and saves those who are crushed in spirit" (Psalm 34:18). This verse has been one of the greatest helps for me personally when I am discouraged. I share it with anyone who has ever lost something or someone and quote it a lot when I am preaching. It is one of those verses that is always true and is supernatural proof of God's love for His kids.

Recently I was speaking with a woman in our church who had just lost her husband after a decades-long marriage. She spoke to me about the incredible sense of loss combined with an overwhelming peace she felt from God in a way she had never known. In her words, she felt as if God was closer to her in those times than ever. She didn't know it, but she was simply testifying to the truth in these verses. God knows just how to comfort a broken heart in ways that humans can't perceive.

Those are five great blessings that the Father bestows on His children. But God knew that His children wouldn't always know how to respond to this kind of fatherly love, so He also gives us bright ideas on ways to receive what we need from Him. Here are some proper responses found in this psalm and other places.

"Seek the Lord while He may be found; call upon Him while He is near," (Isaiah 55:6). Since God answers when I call, first, before I look anywhere else for a solution to a problem, I should seek Him. The prodigal son knew where to find his father, and he pointed his feet in that direction. When you see that word "seek," don't think of it as just looking around.

When we were on road trips with my dad when we were kids, he saw every kind of wildlife each locale had to offer. He would yell, "Brett, see those deer over there? Look, look!" And, of course, since I didn't have my dad's eagle eyes or his passion for hunting deer, I would look up and say, "Where?" We would usually zoom out of range before I ever saw anything. Now, had I been really "seeking" a deer, I would have said, "Dad, stop the car! I must see these deer you speak of!" But since I wasn't that into it, I just looked for two seconds and thought, *Oh, well—Dad has really good eyesight. Maybe next time.*

Seeking is not the same as just looking around for God. Seeking is where I put everything else out of my mind and focus on God and bring my request to Him. Then I silently wait for some kind of direction. I believe many Christians think of seeking God as simply talking at Him. Talking in God's direction is not seeking Him. Seeking Him is praying, then listening until hearing His response.

A lot of good people get confused on this issue. They just don't understand how God communicates to them, so they quit before even starting to seek and listen. Some begin to bring all their problems to other humans who then give their best Oprah imitations and empathize with various kinds of pseudo-spiritual solutions. Seeking God is a little like hunting for lost car keys: you know you're stranded unless you retrieve them, so you hunt and sweat and look without stopping until you find them.

If you're in a tough spot in life right now as you read this, know that God wants to help you. Seek him! Jeremiah 29:13 says, "You will seek me and find me when you seek me with all your heart."

"Glorify the LORD with me; let us exalt his name together" (Psalm 34:3). After you have sought him, make it your goal to glorify him. The writer here is asking us to glorify God, but how does that happen? Well, simply put, I glorify God when I make Him look good.

I think of it like this: when my three girls succeed in life or school or do something nice for someone else, to some degree I share in their glory. By making good choices, they reflect back on my parenting, and they make me look good to others who may be watching. Of course, when they were small and threw fits and rolled on the floor of Wal-Mart as they were being removed from the toy aisle, I was able to pretend I didn't know them.

I can glorify God in many ways, but here are a few to consider. When I am generous with my life, I glorify God. God is always so generous to all of us in the first place, and when I share that quality with the world—for His sake—I make him look good. But I can also glorify God by telling my "God stories" to others. I make Him look good when I remember out loud what God has saved me out of and what He has brought me through.

Recently my mother shared a great God story with me about life before I was born that enriched my faith and glorified God. Her story started in 1946. She told me how as newlyweds she and my father heard from God that they should move from West Virginia to Nashville to attend Trevecca Nazarene College. My Father knew that God wanted him to preach, and he needed to go to school to earn his degree in theology after serving three years in World War II. My dad had a call from God, but they didn't have any money. They also didn't have a car—but God provided a ride to Nashville via their gracious pastor. With one hundred dollars total, the promise of the GI Bill to pay for college, and a newborn baby boy named Greg, they set off to an address.

The address belonged to the only people they knew in Nashville. They had hopes of staying at their home—at least until they could figure out the next step. When they were dropped off, my mom relates that these folks were the poorest people they had ever seen. The man of the house was very kind, but he was disabled and unemployed. It was obvious they couldn't handle company, even for just a night. To amplify the problem, in 1946 all the American GIs were coming home from war and looking for places to live. There weren't many apartments or dormitories to move into, and where could they even go with such limited resources?

As they left the home, the lady of the house felt horrible because she was unable to extend hospitality, but she didn't know what to do. She tried to call for rooms to rent but couldn't find any. So Mom and Dad started walking down the road with no place to go. But then, in a God moment, the woman ran after them and yelled that her sister had a room in her house that might be free. Sure enough, it was the perfect place for my parents to start, right across the street from a brewery and within walking distance of the college. It was a true miracle that God orchestrated.

I can also glorify God by speaking faith words about Him to others. Our culture is very sight-driven and skeptical, and faith is perceived by many to be delusional. But when I speak words of faith about God, and I allow Him to reward my faith publicly, as He always does, then He gets the glory, and the skeptical onlooker may become a curious seeker.

"Taste and see that the LORD is good; blessed is the man who takes refuge in him. Fear the LORD, you his saints, for those who fear him lack nothing" (Psalm 34:8-9). Don't miss this offer! It's like a money-back guarantee. God is saying, "Don't trust somebody else's opinion—taste and see." Many people rely on secondhand information about God instead of learning about Him experientially. I think part of the problem is getting back to my main thought on what kind of God our Father really is. The misconceptions and fears that people have about God are keeping many away from His love and goodness.

Chocolate is one of my favorite things in life. I would love to survive simply on high-protein, no-calorie chocolate, should it be invented. I have had this love as far back as I can remember. But there had to be that first time when my mind took the step of faith and put that brown and blocky substance on my tongue. I had an original "taste and see" moment with chocolate, and life for me was forever changed.

This open invitation from our Father God is to people who are not aware of what He is really like. They are the people who may have heard the bad "God stories," seen weirdness done in His name, and know very few of His followers who seem to reflect a kind of God they would want to follow. But God goes around those objections and just says, "Taste for yourself!"

Dr. Seuss says many of the same things in his great children's book, *Green Eggs and Ham.* The rhyme tells of the character Sam, who is attempting to share his love for this strange breakfast food with a new friend. Sam is relentless, and in the last pages of the book he finally convinces his new friend to try them. The key moment comes when the friend puts this new meal into his mouth and is surprised to find that all his fears were off base. He loves green eggs and ham! And he is thankful for his new friend, Sam.

Obviously, not every new experience is good for us. A drug addict who shares a needle with a new friend, for instance, is in no way being a blessing. But the promise here for any who listen is simply the fact that when you taste and see the Lord, you will find out that He's really good. And without tasting Him for yourself, you can't ever really know Him.

As a way of closing this chapter, let me give you some of my personal impressions of my Heavenly Father that were shaped by my earthly father, Norman Rickey. Norman was a pastor and preacher for more than sixty years, up until a recent heart attack slowed him down. He is a good father in that he loves me and finds ways to express that love both in word and deed. He was also a good pastor. Every week I stand on his shoulders as I preach the Word. For instance, I learned how to be tender from my dad. When my dad preached, he usually shed a tear somewhere in his message. Dad is an emotional and passionate guy. He loves other people, and he hates it when people are in pain. And since he is free to be like that—emotionally vulnerable—so am I. He is still a great source of encouragement on my weekly phone calls. He tells me how proud he is of me; he tells me how much he loves me. He tells me how he prays for me each day and that my life is making him so proud and bringing him a little glory in the process. My dad makes me understand a little bit more about my heavenly dad, and for that I am eternally grateful.

I know that many are not as blessed by their parents as I have been. And there is nothing I can say that will make the pain of a horrible childhood go away. God doesn't wave a magic wand to wipe away the past. But He will enable you to have a better future if you allow Him to. And my invitation to you is simply to seek the real Father of us all, to try Him and taste Him and learn to walk with Him every day. No matter what kind of picture you may have of God from a distance, I can guarantee you this: when you see the Heavenly Father up close and personal, you will see a picture of a Father running with arms wide open in your direction, preparing to give you the best life you could dream of. And after the hugs and kisses comes the party.

Can You Relate?

Read through the following questions and record your thoughts and reactions.

1. Have you ever thought of God as the wizard in *The Wizard of Oz?* Where do you think this view of God as far away, out of touch, and scatterbrained came from? Is there any truth to this view of Him?

_____

_____

_____

_____

_____

_____

_____

_____

_____

_____

_____

_____

_____

_____

2. Brett lays out five things that give him hope in God. What kind of things give you encouragement that God cares personally for you?

_____

_____

_____

_____

_____

_____

_____

_____

_____

_____

_____

_____

_____

_____

_____

_____

_____

_____

_____

3. Do you ever feel as if God doesn't take your call? Have there been instances in your life where you didn't understand the answer right away? Explain.

_____

_____

_____

_____

_____

_____

_____

_____

_____

_____

_____

_____

_____

_____

_____

_____

_____

_____

_____

_____

_____

4. Of the four answers to prayer, which is the hardest for you to receive? Tell about your experience with all four answers.

_____

_____

_____

_____

_____

_____

_____

_____

_____

_____

_____

_____

_____

_____

_____

_____

_____

_____

_____

5. When you get news, whether it's a good grade, promotion, or something else entirely, what is the first thing you do? Do blessings from God make the list of things you're excited to share with others? How do you speak faith words?

_____

_____

_____

_____

_____

_____

_____

_____

_____

_____

_____

_____

_____

_____

_____

_____

_____

_____

6. Have you ever relied on secondhand information and ended up saying or doing something wrong in response to it? How much more important do you think it is to rely on firsthand information about the nature of God when it comes to your relationship with Him and other believers?

_____

_____

_____

_____

_____

_____

_____

_____

_____

_____

_____

_____

_____

_____

_____

_____

EIGHT
HOUSE PARTY

His son said to him, "Father, I have sinned
against both heaven and you, and I am no longer
worthy of being called your son." But his father
said to the servants, "Quick! Bring the finest robe
in the house and put it on him. Get a ring for his
finger and sandals for his feet. And kill the calf
we have been fattening. We must celebrate with a
feast, for this son of mine was dead and has now
returned to life. He was lost, but now
he is found." So the party began.

—Luke 15:21-24, NLT

I like parties, and I like vacations, both of which make me lean toward the idea that vacations and road trips and big bashes are very biblical. You just have to look at what God did when He took the people Israel out of Egypt. He sent them on a big family vacation, all expenses paid. It wasn't supposed to last forty years, but I think a case could loosely be made that God may have wanted these families to bond in the desert before beginning their new lives in the Promised Land. I'm not certain about this interpretation, but it's worth a thought. Even if I'm wrong about the Israelites, though, I'm right to say that I like vacations.

When I think about vacations for me and mine, my mind drifts back to our long drive toward the beach every year—from Oklahoma to the Florida panhandle. We passed through Arkansas, Louisiana, Mississippi, Alabama, and then into Florida on a network of four-lane interstates and winding two-lane highways.

Our hope began to grow as we noticed the salt smell in the air combined with fumes from the refinery as we went over the bay bridge in Mobile, Alabama. I remember driving while filling my mind with the anticipation of lying on the beach with the sound of waves pounding the shore and the sugar-white sand under me. This dream of relaxation and beauty had all of us eager to be on the road for fourteen hours one way. We were driven by an expectation of something wonderful, and when we got there, we were always happy we made the effort to make a memory. The journey—the car ride to Florida—was generally a test of determination and endurance, especially when our three girls were younger. There were fun moments, but also a lot of not-so-fun moments. For instance, the restroom stops in small towns in Arkansas and Mississippi were a whole lot like a jungle adventure—exhilarating and full of potential dangers and unknown diseases at the same time. As time went by, we quickly learned which small towns were serious about their law enforcement and which fast food places were truly fast.

Road trips are usually that way. The future is the fuel for the short-term pain that I am willing to put myself through. Personally, one of my greatest adventures came when I got to explore the Sierra mountain range around Lake Tahoe and Yosemite National Park. I remember entering Yosemite from the northeast entrance. The scenery was beautiful, but not what I was hoping for. I had seen some Ansel Adams black-and-white photos years before, but I really didn't know much about the park or where those photos were taken. For me, part of the adventure of travel is to go off the grid and explore areas as I come upon them, without a rigid plan in place.

Since I was a little underwhelmed so far, I stopped at a ranger station and got a map of the park and an estimate of how far it was to Yosemite Valley. I felt as if this was where I needed to be, but I found out that it would take about another two hours of driving to get there. Since I had already driven three hours, I almost turned around. But the ranger saw my dismay and said, "Oh, you can't turn back now if you've never seen the valley." He had that look in his eye like a person who had just shared a big secret. So I took the nonverbal prodding and drove on.

As I finally completed the valley descent, I remember coming around the final curve where the road opens up and begins to follow the Merced River. I drove back eastward and got my first glimpse of the famous granite monolith, El Capitan, which rises straight up more than three thousand feet from the valley floor. I looked to my right and was overwhelmed by the sight of Bridal Veil Falls. I began to have tears in my eyes, awestruck by the beauty. God usually speaks to me best through natural beauty, and I had never heard God's voice this loudly.

I stopped, parked and walked. I was instantly met with the cedar-like smell of the massive Sequoia redwoods combined with the strong aroma of pine. As I walked toward the river to check it out, I investigated a fallen redwood at least two hundred feet long. The trunk diameter at the base was taller than my reach as it lay on its side. I poked my entire hands in the folds of the extra thick bark that protects these giant trees from forest fires. This one looked as if it had gone down from disease; only God knows for sure. The Merced River was crystal clear, cold, and beautiful. I walked in water up to my knees, and my toes sank into the grayish sand flecked with golden pyrite dust. The smooth rolling of the river was broken only by an occasional trout in search of a meal, nipping the surface.

I took off my shirt and used it as a towel to dry my legs and feet and headed back to the car to drive on to the trail marked "Yosemite Falls." The hiking time was about two hours up, so I went for it. It was a great trail for a novice like me—not too steep—but it still kept me out of breath and made for a great workout.

Again, I wasn't disappointed by what was at the top. To the east I was able to clearly see the most memorable of all of Yosemite's landmarks: the famous mountain known as "Half-Dome." I marveled at the size and scope of it. My mind immediately moved to the psalm where David exclaimed, "What is man, that you are mindful of him?" (Psalm 8:4). I felt so small yet so loved by God both at the same time. That was one of my "greatest ever" days with God.

I hope to go back there one day with my family in tow. It was a life-changing experience that I look forward to repeating and sharing. I now have that glint in my eye that the ranger shared with me. I know a secret, but I will gladly share it with anyone who listens. I have already been back many times in my imagination, smelled the redwoods and bristlecone pines and felt the crisp mountain breeze on my face. I can't go there physically right now, but in my mind I can—anytime.

Our God has given us this great potential to imagine our eternal destination. I know you probably are like me and try not to think about death too much, but every once in a while it's good to remember that life on this earth is just a flash—just a breath—compared to eternity. You and I will spend far more time over there, wherever there is, than here on the earth as it is.

One of my big concerns is that too many people who love Jesus are living life and forgetting there is an even better life to come. They just never stop and prepare for heaven. Worse yet, there are others who don't know or follow Jesus who are trying to fill their lives with temporary pleasures, trying to stay busy, or just numbing themselves from the pain of life. They are not living a life of purpose but simply floundering after what feels good in the moment.

Let me be clear. I want to help you think about the fact that all of humanity is on a journey. I know it sounds corny, but it's true. We are not home yet. And for followers of Jesus, it's like what the old Sinatra song says—the best is yet to come!

In the story of the prodigal son, there is a celebration given by the father. It's a party with great food and fun and music. And the story of the celebration points us in the direction of the ultimate feast that one day all of God's children will share. It's a place we call heaven or paradise, but one day all believers will simply call it home.

The apostle Paul helps us look forward to the new life we will have one day by saying,

> We know that when these bodies of ours are taken down like tents and folded away, they will be replaced by resurrection bodies in heaven—God-made, not handmade—and we'll never have to relocate our "tents" again. Sometimes we can hardly wait to move—and so we cry out in frustration. Compared to what's coming, living conditions around here seem like a stopover in

an unfurnished shack, and we're tired of it! We've been given a glimpse of the real thing, our true home, our resurrection bodies! The Spirit of God whets our appetite by giving us a taste of what's ahead. He puts a little of heaven in our hearts so that we'll never settle for less. *(2 Corinthians 5:1-5 TM)*

So what will Heaven be like? Jesus promised his disciples; "In my Father's house are many rooms; if it were not so, I would have told you. I am going there to prepare a place for you" (John 14:2). Whatever heaven is like, it will be something that is unbelievably appealing. If Jesus is preparing us an eternal home, I believe it will also be incredibly fulfilling.

For instance, when I go home, my mom makes cherry cheese pie. She has prepared a meal just for me. She knows what I like. It's the same reason she doesn't fix me sweet potatoes. And our God understands how we are wired, because He wired us, and He knows what will ultimately prove to be satisfying. I believe what I just wrote. But it is also a statement of faith since I've never been there and don't know anyone who has been there that I trust with one-hundred-percent certainty.

One of the most difficult things to wrap my mind around is eternity. You are probably a lot like me in that I just can't really imagine it very well. I am finite. I have a birthday and a death day to come. Eternity is something I don't understand. I know that eternity goes both ways, back in time and forward in time, and that freaks me out a little bit. However, the Bible does give us all some rich imagery about what heaven will be like. And even though these verses are much debated as to the specifics, there are four agreed-upon truths about our heavenly home that do bring me hope. I've even created an acrostic that spells HOME that I've learned from the last two chapters in the Bible to help you remember.

Heaven is—

Holy

Open to all

Magnificent

Eternity with Jesus.

Heaven Is Holy

The apostle John, writing about the inspired vision of the future he was receiving from God, says this:

> Then I saw a new heaven and a new earth, for the first heaven and the first earth had passed away, and there was no longer any sea. I saw the Holy City, the new Jerusalem, coming down out of heaven from God, prepared as a bride beautifully dressed for her husband. And I heard a loud voice from the throne saying, "Now the dwelling of God is with men, and he will live with them. They will be his people, and God himself will be with them and be their God. He will wipe every tear from their eyes. There will be no more death or mourning or crying or pain, for the old order of things has passed away." *(Revelation 21:1-4)*

The first words used to describe our final home are "the Holy City." The new heaven will be a place where men and women will be able to dwell with a holy God and not feel unworthy. They will have been made holy by Christ, and since heaven is a holy place, sin won't be allowed in. The old order of things will be gone.

On this earth everyone is still susceptible to the current order of things. Sin is allowed to have great power in the world, and the enemy does have ability to destroy and deceive men and women. As a result of sin in the world, men and women mistreat one another, they steal from one another, they envy one another, they lie to one another, and on and on. Sin is in the world and in humanity, and death is a certainty to every human being.

As Christians, we understand that in Christ something new has happened. The kingdom of God has come, partially but not entirely. The new heaven will be the kingdom of God fully revealed on earth as it is in heaven. Sin and its effects on humanity that result in sickness and sadness will evaporate. John reminds us that this holiness will be forever. "Nothing impure will ever enter it, nor will anyone who does what is shameful or deceitful, but only those whose names are written in the Lamb's book of life" (Revelation 21:27).

Since our world is as broken as it is, it's hard to conceive of a place without striving, competition, hunger, anger, angst, fear, or worry. Heaven, being a holy place, assures me that those things will be absent.

Heaven Is Open to All

He who was seated on the throne said, "I am making everything new!" Then he said, "Write this down, for these words are trustworthy and true." He said to me: "It is done. I am the Alpha and the Omega, the Beginning and the End. To him who is thirsty I will give to drink without cost from the spring of the water of life" *(Revelation 21:5-6)*

Verse six gives the qualification for God's eternal water of life: thirst. I have never met a person who didn't know what thirst was all about. Around the world, since clean water is scarce, physical thirst is a real problem. Thirst is something we instinctively seek to deal with the moment our bodies whisper, "Get me some liquid now."

Thirst implies desperation. When a person is thirsty, it is hard for him or her to think about anything else. I have noticed that heaven comes to earth for those who get really thirsty for the presence of God and seek after Him like nothing else. I am convinced that the reason the Church in the United States is so powerless is that its people are not desperately thirsty enough to search for the only source that will satisfy their souls. I am constantly amazed at the high level of brokenness that exists even in good families. Jesus will always deliver the truly desperate and reward them with His presence. In the prodigal story, and even in the exodus of Israel from Egypt, we see this common thread. Desperation always precedes deliverance. Jesus once said, "Blessed are those who hunger and thirst for righteousness, for they will be filled" (Matthew 5:6).

So heaven is reserved not just for the good people in life; it is reserved for those who come freely to Jesus to quench their thirsty souls. As the prodigal story points out, all a person has to do is point his or her life back toward the Father and humble himself or herself and ask for forgiveness. The party is for anyone and everyone who will call on the name of the Lord for rescue.

But John also goes on to describe some terrific heavenly scenery to look forward to as well.

Heaven Is Magnificent

As you read these words slowly, let your imagination and the Holy Spirit build you a picture:

> I did not see a temple in the city, because the Lord God Almighty and the Lamb are its temple. The city does not need the sun or the moon to shine on it, for the glory of God gives it light, and the Lamb is its lamp. *(Revelation 21:22-23)*

I once wrote a sermon I titled "Brightland" that I built around these verses. I imagined a place where light was not reflected from the plants and animals but actually emanated from them. In that world, every living thing would be the true inhabitation, rather than the reflection, of almighty God. I got this idea when I thought back on the time in the Bible when it talks about Moses meeting with God, and his face literally glowed for a short time.

If that was the result of a short-term visit, I am nearly certain that our eternal beauty will be the glory of God seen through our new immortalized features. I believe we will know one another and see each as God truly designed us to be seen, not like the facade that we usually show the world now.

Sometime back our family took a trip to Disney World. We took pictures at every stop, because Mindy said so. I think it's a good idea to listen to Mindy. Something struck me that's already obvious to most, but I'm slow, so it cracked me up. What got me laughing was that my picture smile is not really me smiling. It's me pretending to smile. The really big, goofy smiling me is not fit for photos. And sure enough, my whole family is cursed like this. Every one of us has a picture smile and then a real smile. In heaven, there won't be any picture smiling happening. God's glory will be shining bright and clear, and that will be pretty cool. However, the final element that John saved for last is really the best part of heaven in my mind.

Heaven Means Spending Eternity with Jesus

Then the angel showed me the river of the water of life, as clear as crystal, flowing from the throne of God and of the Lamb down the middle of the great street of the city. On each side of the river stood the tree of life, bearing twelve crops of fruit, yielding its fruit every month. And the leaves of the tree are for the healing of the nations. No longer will there be any curse. The throne of God and of the Lamb will be in the city, and his servants will serve him. They will see his face, and his name will be on their foreheads. There will be no more night. They will not need the light of a lamp or the light of the sun, for the Lord God will give them light. And they will reign for ever and ever. *(Revelation 22:1-5)*

In this passage, verse 3 tells us what we will be doing in heaven: we will be serving Jesus. And verse 5 tells us what our rank or position over creation will be: we will be reigning with Him.

Isn't that an odd thought? Heaven isn't a retirement destination—it's a place where a person will still be serving. In fact, I believe it will be pure joy to serve him. I believe that serving is what His followers will truly long to do and what each of us was made to do. It will be a passionate connection to completely serve the one we love—Jesus. Somehow in doing that we also will reign with Him. I'm not sure what that means, but even after we die and are immortalized, creation moves ahead, and we will take our place. But one day I do long to hear Jesus say, "Come, you who are blessed by my Father; take your inheritance, the kingdom prepared for you since the creation of the world" (Matthew 25:34).

C. S. Lewis in the final page of his last book of *The Chronicles of Narnia* series, *The Last Battle*, describes the crossing over into heaven:

For us this is the end of all the stories. . . . But for them it was only the beginning of the real story. All their life in this world . . . had only been the cover and the title page; now at last they were beginning Chapter One of the Great Story, which no one on earth has read, which goes on forever and in which every chapter is better than the one before.

As you read this, I know your life may not be where you want it to be. My charge to you is to begin to engage your imagination on occasion. Start facing your life toward the future, no matter how difficult your past may have been, and begin to live in light of eternity. The writer of Hebrews reminds us "For this world is not our home; we are looking forward to our everlasting home in heaven, (Hebrews 13:14, TLB).

When you really understand the brevity of life on this side and the fact that this world isn't our home for very long, it can help when facing the hardships and changes that come to every life.

The house party is the end of the prodigal story. The lost son finally makes it home and takes his place again. There is no condemnation or finger-pointing, just the loving embrace of the father and the joyful celebration of a family who has rediscovered its lost child.

Our Heavenly Father is all about parties. And if you're reading this and feel distant from Him today, you don't have to feel that way. You can begin to live eternal life right now. You don't have to wait until you die to experience it. You can have true fellowship with God and His family simply by talking to the Father. If you want to, I've included a prayer that you can pray to get started on this journey, or you can pray it if you are just wanting to return back home. If you pray this prayer, your problems won't all instantly disappear; but when you pray this prayer, you are taking the first steps back home. Like a boomerang, you are back where you belong.

Father, I understand that the world I see is temporary, and I believe that my soul will live forever. I want to live with you in heaven one day, and I understand that your Son, Jesus, is the path to get there. I commit to follow Him for the rest of my days on this earth, and I look forward to seeing you face to face and living in your presence forever. In Jesus' name I pray. Amen.

Can You Relate?

Read through the following questions and record your thoughts and reactions.

1. Brett described various road trips and said that "future is the fuel for the short-term pain." Have you ever felt this way in life? What kind of road trip are you on? What is your destination?

_____

_____

_____

_____

_____

_____

_____

_____

_____

_____

_____

_____

_____

_____

_____

2. Yosemite National Park was a glimpse of what heaven
   will be like to Brett. Have you ever experienced a glimpse
   of heaven? What do you think heaven will be like?

_____

_____

_____

_____

_____

_____

_____

_____

_____

_____

_____

_____

_____

_____

_____

_____

_____

_____

3. In Genesis 5 we are told that Enoch was so close to God that he was taken to be with Him and never died. Do you think Enoch experienced some of the holiness of heaven? In what way?

_____

_____

_____

_____

_____

_____

_____

_____

_____

_____

_____

_____

_____

_____

_____

_____

_____

_____

_____

4. Why do you think Christians in American churches aren't desperate for God? Have you ever been desperate for a breakthrough from God? How was that time different from typical difficult situations?

_____

_____

_____

_____

_____

_____

_____

_____

_____

_____

_____

_____

_____

_____

_____

_____

_____

_____

5. Brett says that in heaven "we will know one another and see each as God truly designed us to be seen." Have you ever struggled with being two-faced? What do you think it will be like to be perfect, with only one side of yourself? Do you even really know yourself well enough to imagine what you will be like in heaven?

_____

_____

_____

_____

_____

_____

_____

_____

_____

_____

_____

_____

_____

_____

_____

_____

_____

_____

6. How do you think we can both serve Jesus and reign with Him in heaven? What could we possibly do to help the world's only perfect man?

_____

_____

_____

_____

_____

_____

_____

_____

_____

_____

_____

_____

_____

_____

_____

_____

_____

_____

_____

NOTES

Chapter 2

1. J. C. Ryle, *Holiness: Its Nature, Hindrances, Difficulties and Roots* (Welwin, Hertfordshire, England: Evangelical Press, 1985).

Chapter 3

1. <www.seniorjournal.com/NEWS/abing/5>. Site now discontinued.

Chapter 6

1. <www.theledger.com/article/20101016/NEWS/10175007/1021/life?p=1&tc=pg>.

RETHINK YOUR LIMITS

No one likes to be told what to do. No one enjoys having limits placed on his or her personal freedom—especially when they are drawn for us by others who present them as interpretations of religious faith. *Stay in the Yard* is not a book that promotes legalism or seeks to reestablish a puritanical approach to faith. It helps readers identify a new source of hope in God's Word and strengthen their faith by recognizing that commitment to obedience is the only way to truly enjoy abundant life.

STAY IN THE YARD
Rethinking the Limits of Personal Freedom / Brett Rickey

BEACON HILL PRESS
OF KANSAS CITY

www.beaconhillbooks.com | facebook.com/beaconhillpress

Available online and wherever books are sold.

FOCUS

Our culture is obsessed with being "cool." Many people,
even Christians, strive for the next big thing, the newest look,
and the most impressive accomplishment. As a result, their
lives are overscheduled, overworked, and filled with debt—
and they have very little to show for it. In *Chasing Cool,* Brett
Rickey exposes the attitudes and misconceptions that often
contribute to many of our actions and desires and helps us
rediscover what our true pursuits should be and recognize
the abundant life Christ has given us.

CHASING COOL
Examining the Pursuits of Your Heart / Brett Rickey

Why Whole? W.H.O.L.E. was birthed in October 2018 after a painful and disappointing dating experience and extreme exhaustion, burnout, idolatry, and anxiety as a result of workaholism. I was deeply depressed and suicidal because I wholeheartedly believed that God plus someone and something made me whole. It was not until I came to the end of myself that He opened my eyes and heart to the overwhelming peace, joy, and steadfast love that was there for me all along.

As a single woman and teacher, it is my aim to help women of all ages and backgrounds to find their fulfillment in the Lord and Him alone. My aim is to help teachers, schools, and fragile women and girls pursue Christ and His wholeness. I want people to know, experience, and live out the Gospel. This organization was established to provide resources, assistance, and encouragement to schools, teachers, churches, women, and girls.

"What Happens When A Black Girl Doesn't Feel Like Magic?" is a book that came from that painful experience. God wants us to run to Him when the sadness and pressures of life become overwhelming. He brings us the love, joy, and peace that we all long for.

What Happens When A Black Girl Doesn't Feel Like Magic? by Chaquana M. Muhammad Townsend

When a black girl doesn't feel like magic, she hides behind her successes and finds her significance in performance. She's smart enough to know that people only call you "magic" when you are performing and living up to their standard. She masks her discomfort and pain with a "Never Let Them See You Struggle Mentality" because after all, her black is magic, right?

Her magic comes with a hidden fight to believe God loves the sinner who was discarded and taken advantage of continuously. This black girl fights to believe that if Jesus saw her daily struggle to love, to stay pure, to show His love to others, He would hide His face in rejection. What if anxiety makes this black girl feel less magical? What if academic success and being the best only fuel the loss of "Black Girl Magic?"

What if we could reverse what "Black Girl Magic" really is? Could we add the pain and successes into the equation? What if my "Black Girl Magic" came with wounds and scars that still needed ointment from time to time? What if it came with beauty that was deeper than a degree or financial success? What if it came with truth, honesty, rawness, ratchetness, and excellence all at the same time? Would it still be magical?

"Black Girl Magic" is Harriet Tubman, Maya Angelou, Oprah Winfrey, the R&B Legend and Queen Mary J. Blige along with the countless women who have seen and overcome the highs and lows of this life! Women who have seen the struggle, yet they contain to soar! Pain and
beauty sit at their doorstep only to create more beauty because "Black Girl Magic" is the ability to get up even when you don't want to . It's the ability to keep fighting when life has knocked you out! It is freedom, victory, triumph, and persevering through the rain. We are "Black Girl Magic!"

Table of Contents

Acknowledgements

First, I want to acknowledge my Lord and Savior Jesus Christ. He is the very reason why I am here and why I am able to go on each and everyday. He is my healing balm, and my comforter in and through every trial. He is my ultimate King, lover, and ruler, and I am so grateful to be His. He has truly restored my innermost being! I will live for Him because He deserves it.

Second, I want to thank my friends, family, and church family for being there for me. I am grateful for every person who has encouraged me, prayed for me, and lived in a way that pointed me to Jesus. Thank you to my best friend Kellee for being my ride or die partner for life. Shout out to my mother, father, sister, brothers, and beautiful nieces and nephews. I love you guys!

Lastly, thank you to those who have supported me in dance, teaching, and writing this book. Thank you for encouraging me through the writing process. May God bless you all! This book would not be here without you. I am forever grateful!

Foreword

Keelan Adams, Associate Pastor of Flatline Church at Chisolm:

This work paints a beautiful picture of God's providence, redemption, sanctification, and a little girl who grows into a woman that looks back and sees God's sovereign hand of protection over her entire life. This is an "open book" of sorts into the deep chambers of the author's heart. Herein, women can learn lessons from the implications of each mistake and error. On the other hand, this work issues a clarion call for men to take note of biblical manhood with the stark contrast of manhood run amuck. Altogether, this book helps both men and women see their intrinsically depraved condition and throughout introduces them to the only Savior who is able to provide a remedy for such ailments. His name is Jesus!

Alonzo Brown, Associate Pastor of Strong Tower at Washington:

Chaquana is one of the most authentic and sensitive people I know! In this book, Chaquana does a good job taking you through the dark roads she has traveled and bringing the reader to come away with enormous hope! This easy read has a sad reality...her story is common amongst a lot of people. The difference with her experiences is though she's traveled down these dark, familiar roads many have traveled, another wonderful story unfolds from a purposeful and loving Father who is there giving power and most importantly, Himself. Chaquana's story says we are never alone, even in our darkest valleys because we have a Savior who understands exactly where we are through His own personal experiences. He turns our dark roads to highways of healing and light! Great job Quani!

LONGING TO BE LOVED/CHILDHOOD

One of my deepest desires and deepest flaw is the desire to be wanted and loved. I have learned a few things about myself over the years: I am loyal, deeply committed, and consistent even when I don't get the same thing in return. I desired these things growing up; however, I never got them from the people I valued the most. My story and upbringing are a clear sign and testament of a young girl starved for affection. I was born on October 15, 1988 in Bronx, New York. I was born to a crack addicted mother and an abusive father. My father's verbal abuse showed itself when I finally started a relationship with him in my teens, but my mother experienced his physical and mental abuse. I was three pounds and eleven ounces due to my mother's drug addiction. My sister Nikki and I were both born premature, yet we grew into healthy young women. My sister and I are eleven months apart. I also have two older brothers, David and Benjamin. We were born in the 80's, but the 90's era had a hold on us! We loved SWV, Mary J. Blige, Mariah Carey, Biggie Smalls, and the list goes on and on. Since we lived in both New York and New Orleans during our younger years, we were music heads and I was the natural dancer. Life in both places was fun, but it also brought on challenges that caused deep wounds and scars that still plague me today. I had beliefs and values as a believer that the Lord has completely changed and restored; nonetheless, I am still recovering even at 29 venturing into 30.

Growing up, my sister and I were inseparable. In other words, we were never apart, literally. We are like night and day. Csniqua is like fire, and Chaquana is like ice! I remember a teacher in high school pointing out the clear difference in our personalities. I was overly obedient and rarely got into trouble. My sister, on the other hand, was outspoken and fearless! She was the popular girl, and I was the nerd who hung out with Asians, Hispanics, and Blacks. I loved reading and writing because it was one of the places I felt the safest. My brothers lived with us as well; however, one of my brothers moved to New York to live with his father. My mother has four children, two girls and two boys. I am the youngest child. My world was turned upside down at a very young age. I was only four. One day, I got the bright idea to take a lighter and light a mattress just for fun. My grandmother came in the room to put out the flame with water, but it was too late. Her hand was burned slightly, and we lost our home. We moved into a shelter, and then we finally moved to New Orleans to be near my great uncle. My grandmother became our sole provider while my mother stayed in New York for several years.

New Orleans was the number one murder capital in 1992. We lived in the 9th ward, and it had its challenges. My grandmother did an amazing job at affirming her grandchildren in every way. I told her I wanted to be a doctor, and she called me her future doctor. She never talked down to us, and her encouragement helped me to excel in school. She slipped up once and called me stupid for my actions when I was being disobedient and immediately apologized. She was present with homework, school activities, and graduations, yet I was longing for the love of mother and father. Although she was my hero and an angel on earth, she couldn't heal the void of affirmation and acceptance that I craved from my parents.

It's funny how children cry out for love and acceptance in so many ways. I never felt pretty enough, small enough, or smart enough because I longed to hear it from my parents. I remember talking to my Dad once when I moved to New Orleans. When I was a little girl, I remember him buying sundresses for Nikki and me. I was so happy to receive and wear that dress. When it came to my mother, I remember having dreams, tantrums, and long bouts of crying because I just wanted a mother's love and touch.

My mom decided to come to New Orleans to stay for sometime, and it was okay. Although Nikki and I were happy she was there, we soon realized she didn't know how to parent us. We were very afraid of her because she didn't play with us; however, we knew in our hearts that our grandmother played the better role of a mother. She gave us so much love and care. We never went without anything! Christmas was my favorite time of the year because she made it so worth it! The presents that we desired were received, and we loved the whole idea of gifts! I never missed a meal, and I was cared for so tenderly. Nonetheless, I had a complex. I was overweight and filled with fear and shame due to sexual abuse.

I love the phrase, "Black Girl Magic"; however, that magic

never really resonated with me. From the time I was four all the way up to the present, I have always fought to believe I was worth loving. It's funny how one moment and multiple acts of sin committed against you, can cause you to think that something is inherently wrong with you. Now, I don't want to play the victim role because I am aware of the reality of being born a sinner. However, as a young girl with inconsistent parents and circumstances beyond my control, I learned to dance and become friends with shame. I was four or five when I first encountered a young man. I remember it like it happened the other day.

I was playing on the bed with a t-shirt and panties on, innocently rolling on the bed. A friend of my older brother looked at me and pointed towards my lower parts. He asked, "What's that?" I looked at him and smiled. I knew what he was saying, but I knew it was wrong. He asked could he touch me, and I said yes. In that moment, as a young girl, I felt wanted and taken advantage of at the same time. I liked the attention, but I hated what it cost me. I wish I could say it was the first and last time it happened, but I became numb to young men touching me and calling me beautiful. Everytime it happened, I never said stop. I let them have their way carrying the guilt and shame with me. I remember flirting with an older man at a birthday party after being molested the first time. My oldest brother walked into my room and stated loudly, "Quani, I heard you were acting like a hoe!" I was five at the time. I crawled under my bed and cried. That was the first time in my life that I vividly remember hating myself and wishing I could disappear. The self-hate began right after that.

I learned a core belief at a very young age: "You have something that men want." The sexual abuse caused me to want men and hate them at the same time. I didn't feel safe with them. My dad wasn't around until I turned 14. I would fantasize about having children minus the father being there because that was all I knew. Even as a young girl, I internalized giving women a try because I felt so unsure of man's ability to love me and stick around. What hurt the most about the abuse was a sad reality: I knew these men because they were friends of the family and one happened to be a cousin. During my elementary school years, I experimented with a girl amongst other things. I vividly remember watching a porn my brother had lying around. I remember humping objects and a girl in particular. I showed her my lower parts, and she showed me hers. I thought it was fun, but the enemy gave me a taste of the other side. It felt safer than a man, so we fooled around a couple of times. I still liked boys, but women caught my eye and attention too.

I can recall being head over heels over a guy named Justin, a friend of my brother. In my mind, he was the finest thing I had ever seen! He had beautiful caramel skin, and I could stare at him forever. My heart and stomach went crazy every time he was around. One day, I got the courage to write him a note. It said these alarming words: "I like you. Do you like me? Check yes or no." After he read the note, he ripped it up and threw it on the ground. My heart was crushed by this teenage boy who rightfully rejected a young girl in elementary school. The experience of molestation and neglectful parents left me insecure and longing for affirmation and love. I performed academically to show how worthy I was to be loved, but inwardly I felt like damaged goods and firmly believed I was rejected by my parents and abused by men because something was wrong with me.

NO VOICE

Believing you have "no voice" is a learned belief. It started with a moment, a comment, an unintentional act that altered the mind of a young Queen longing to fly. In every instance of my life, I believed my voice and opinion didn't **matter**. I hid my insecurities behind performance because I never felt good enough. Let me explain: I walked around with a secret and painful reminder in my heart. I honestly believed that if people knew about the abuse and rejection I experienced, they would run away like my Mommy and Daddy.

I rarely stood up for myself, and I was shy most of the time. I was bullied, talked about, and taken advantage of because I didn't have the courage to say: "No, you will not mistreat me." Why would I speak up? I allowed myself to be a doormat since I was four, and I watched my grandmother do the same thing for years. My personality and demeanor is just like the woman who raised me. People can sense my sweet, caring, and overly compensating spirit from a mile away. Most of the men I have dated admired me because of my "submissive and quiet" spirit. Children learn to imitate what they see.

I watched my grandmother raise myself and my siblings along with her great grandchildren. I watched her give her all to a church that took advantage of her kindness. She never said no even if it cost her in the end. Yes, it cost her. She dealt with disrespect and disobedience from rebellious children and grandchildren. Despite how people treated her, I never witnessed my grandmother lash out or turn into a monster. She kept her cool and loved people anyway.

However, I wonder if she ever hurt or grew tired. Her love towards people reminded me of water coming from a fountain; it just didn't stop. I wonder if she cried at night when we would wake up and her car would be gone. I wonder if she cried when my brother continued to take her car and dabble in the streets. I wonder if she cried when I would kick and scream and tell her mean things when I didn't get my way. She never really spoke up, and when she did speak, she spoke with grace. Ironically, although she had the most beautiful soul I have ever witnessed, I knew she hurt. Her lack of sharing her "voice" transferred over to me.

The main motivation behind being a "yes" girl or rarely saying no comes from a detrimental belief: "If I say no, they will reject or dislike me. My deepest fear is to be rejected or disliked so to avoid experiencing those emotions and reactions from others, I will comply even when I don't want to." The Lord sees it as being a slave to man and fearing people above Him. It will keep you ensnared, always trying to make others happy when there is safety in the Lord (Proverbs 29:25). My desire to please cost me more than I imagined.

My low-self worth and self-hatred led me to trying marijuana and having sex at 14. Although my sexual life was short lived, and I have been celibate for 13 years. I have compromised in other ways. My first mutual sexual encounter was with a man who was 7 years older than me. I wasn't head over heels or even attracted to him. Everybody was having sex, and he happened to show me some attention like the men from my childhood. I literally remember what I was thinking the night I lost my virginity: "This is probably the only man that will ever want me. He's wasting his time anyway. Nobody else wants me." Do you hear this worthlessness? Do you hear the heart of a young woman who does not see her beauty and value? I hated looking in the mirror because it reminded me that I was a reject. I felt so rejected by my parents that I internalized being an abomination to the outside world.

At 13 and 14, my sister and I sat down with my grandmother and she shared some exciting news with us!! After 9 years of being in New Orleans, we were headed back to New York to live with my mother. We were so excited; however, my grandmother gave us a warning: "It will not be what you think it's going to be." I never knew my mother was on drugs or that I was born a "crack baby" until we made it to New York in 2001. We moved to New York in the summer of 2001.

Shortly after we got there, my mother began using drugs again. My mother would use her food stamp money to buy drugs, steal the money our grandmother would send to us, and have other addicts in and out of the house. My mother eventually became physically abusive, and we had to be taken away from her. One day, my mother became so angry that she dragged me, pulled my hair out, kicked and punched me. I didn't have the courage to hit my own mother, so I took the beating. I remember being deeply hurt and confused by her actions. I didn't understand how a mother could verbally and physically hurt her children.

After the incident, I called my dad to pick me up. I remember it so clearly because once I got into my father's car, he looked at me and jokingly stated, "My poor baby." He made a mockery of my tears and showed no compassion for my hurt. I immediately stopped crying and accepted a false belief that day, "Crying is a weakness." Even as a newly 30 year old woman, crying in front of others is extremely hard for me. Every time the tears fall, I wonder if my vulnerability will be seen as a weakness.

I was 14 and my sister was 15 when we lived with my dad. It is utterly mind-boggling and amazing how the power of a dad can crush or elevate the minds of his children. It is a clear picture of the power of our Heavenly father. His love, grace, and goodness can elevate and crush us at the same time. However, his crushing and discipline produces character, hope, godliness, and perseverance. My father's presence and authority was strong in our home. He was the leader, and we were called to submit to his authority. We cooked, cleaned, and washed clothes. He taught us how to serve and comply to the wishes of a man.

Looking back on that experience, my father created a sense of reverence, fear, and awe in me for the male species. I don't have a hard time respecting and serving a man because it was ingrained in me to do so. However, my father also left painful writings on the wall of my heart that took me a while to overcome. One day he told me these painful words, "You will never be anything. You will be just like your mother." I don't recall why he said those to me. I don't remember being disobedient, yet those words stung. It hurt so bad and all I could do was cry. I didn't want to be on drugs and neglect my children. I can't imagine abandoning and abusing my children. I wanted more out of life, and my own father didn't see that. Stupid and broad were my nicknames. My father was an angry man, and my sister and I experienced his anger on a regular basis. As a result, I was insecure, gullible, and fell prey to the lies and whims of young boys and men. I just wanted somebody to love and accept me as a teenage girl, so I felt refuge in good friends, writing, reading, and poetry.

In high school, I was apart of the geek squad! My best friend was a light-skinned, curvy, skinny, and down-to earth Puerto-Rican beauty named MB. There were also three other girls I hung out with. MB and I were tight, and we loved the idea of being loved! We talked about love and boys all of the time, and we had a personal journal we would pass around between classes. We shared our frustrations, pain, and boredom with school. However, we found safety in writing down our feelings and listening to poetry.

It was a way of escape, and it felt exhilarating! Our journal entries sounded like diaries, and a way to hide our own miseries. In our journal entries, we shared our struggles with boys. It's crazy to read and hear how desperate I was for attention, and how naive I was to ill-intentioned young men. However, even at 30, there are some traits of that naivety still with me. My first journal entry was about a boy named D. He was a 16 year old Crip from Brooklyn. He was fine as wine with hazel brown eyes and a gorgeous smile! When I saw him, I couldn't stop staring. We connected instantly, and I visited Brooklyn frequently. My weakness even to this day is a good-looking man, and D. was a good-looking young brother with pretty eyes, a gorgeous face, and a beautiful smile. I was so glad that something that fine swung my way. I was hooked from the first interaction which led to phone conversations, hanging out, and eventually sex.

Right after we had sex, the phone conversations stopped and the avoidance began. I knew I played the fool. Moreover, he had a secret that he kept from me. He had chlamydia and gonorrhea. When I used the bathroom one day and I was hurting continually, I grew concerned. I went to the doctor and found out I had contracted a sexually transmitted disease. I was shocked because I believed D. when he said he was clean and didn't have anything. This painful experience led me to writing to my best friend MB whom I trusted and loved so deeply. I was longing to see D. after our sexual encounter, so I shared it with her:

I don't know why, but I just wanna see him again. I'm still not calling him until he calls me. I don't know why, but I just can't let it go personally. I think that he's doing it on purpose. He probably thinks he's too good for me. Well, if he calls me, which I highly doubt, I'll say, "Am I your girlfriend and are you my boyfriend?" If he says yes, then it will go on from there. If he says no then that's it. I doubt if he says no, but if he does, what can I do about it. Those eyes, damn those lips (mmm….). I want him so badly, but I know deep down inside I can't. He got me SPEECHLESS!

I was a lost Queen desperate for a young King to love me

who didn't know what love was. Puppy love, butterflies in your stomach kind of "love." We had no solid foundation, and were in heat kind of "love." Needless to say, my older sister Nikki talked to D., and his words were, "She knew what she was getting herself into." He didn't care. I was a hit on the hit list, and praise the Lord I didn't end up pregnant or with an incurable disease. Even during those times of hopelessness, lust, and confusion, God still protected me. MB and I wrote a lot in that journal because we trusted one another. We needed an outlet as we made sense of the crazy world around us. We eventually started going to Barnes and Nobles to read books in the aisles. Next, it was the Nuyorican Cafe in Manhattan and other poetry slams. We loved writing because it gave us a voice and helped us to make sense of everything around us.

During that time, we listened to conscious artists like Immortal Technique and Dead Prez. We gawked over amazing poets and artists who spoke their mind. I found a safe haven, and I used it to share my story with a Foster Care magazine called *Represent*. This magazine showed me that a creative young girl from the Bronx is indeed a writer, and her story and fight to live gives her purpose! After working with that magazine company, I knew I wanted to be a writer. I wrote poetry, dramas, and plays years later, but it started in high school when my mind was open to the world of reading and writing.

I had three dedicated teachers in high school that I remember vividly. One of the teachers names, I can't recall, but he was a white man who so happened to be my P.E. coach. He was always kind, and I remember him telling me that he wanted to see me do well and make it. His words were passionate, genuine, and strong! I will never forget those words because I knew it came from a sincere place. Real recognizes real. In other words, real people recognize genuine spirits, and his spirit resonated with me that day. My P.E. coach wanted me to soar, and I appreciated his passion. One thing about inner-city kids, our senses are very keen to bullcrap and sincere people. We can sniff out the real from the fake in a few seconds. We have to learn to be on the alert. We are forced to become skilled at navigating through the sticky and often hostile forest of the hood. My next two favorite teachers were Mr. Lawson and Ms. Williams. They were African American teachers who were passionate about Economics and African American History. They were excited to see us come into the classroom, and we were treated with so much respect and dignity as students. Mr. Lawson kept in touch with my sister and I outside of school, and he even took us to eat one afternoon. These two teachers became a safe place for my sister and I, and as grown women, we remember their love and investment.

Looking back over my life and childhood, I always felt an inner ache and belief that life had more to offer. It's funny how as an unbeliever I still had God's hand of protection on my life even as His enemy. Every situation and step was ordered and directed by the Lord. I knew I was different, but little did I know, the God of the universe was preparing me for a right relationship with Him. Your past is a gift and a blessing which ultimately points you to a God who will never leave you alone if you belong to Him.

INSECURITY

"You will never be enough" is a phrase I have told myself more times than I should have. There were a few moments in middle school and high school that revealed a sad reality: I was willing to do anything for love even if it cost me my dignity. I went to middle school in New Orleans, and I tried my best to stay out of trouble. I was in middle school in the early 2000's, and New Orleans was known for its crime and constant murders. I vividly remember receiving the news that one of my elementary school teachers was murdered. I was in complete shock! I couldn't comprehend how another human being can so heartlessly take another person's life.

In middle school, I wanted to be accepted and seen as beautiful. I wore makeup to enhance "my beauty"; however, I wished I wasn't overweight and more boys liked me. It's funny how African Americans promote and reinforce colorism in their own communities. New Orleans was known for favoring and uplifting light-skinned women while the brown and dark-skinned women took a back seat. I heard "Say Red!" more times than I wanted to hear. It proved to me that light skin women were more valued and seen as prettier even when some dark skinned girls looked better.

I was definitely "thick" for my age as an eleven year old in middle school. It was clear that I didn't miss a meal, and the food in New Orleans kept my taste buds churning. My mom visit here and there and eventually she stayed for sometime. In the time she would visit and when she did live with us for an extended period of time, I don't recall being called beautiful. She loved to mention how slim and attractive my sister was, and it made me dislike myself even more. I remember writing in my journal, " My mother doesn't love me because I am fat and ugly." I was determined to get the weight off in order to win her over and get the attention of young boys and men.

I starved myself literally. I barely ate, and I ran up and down the stairs in my home constantly. I remember one of our neighbors who happened to be a boy told me, "Quani, you would have dudes all over you if you lost some weight." His comment added fuel to the fire, and in one summer, I went from a size fourteen to a size four. My grandmother didn't know I was starving myself until one morning as I headed to school. I walked unto the bus to pay my fare, and as soon as I put the money in the machine, everything went black. I passed out on the bus, and my grandmother was called immediately. She took me to Shoney's Restaurant and encouraged me to eat. I needed that moment of understanding, and right after that, I became healthier and more stable. I began to eat more; however, I was still skinny because of the drastic weight loss. I dropped 10 dress sizes, so it took me a while to get that weight back.

During my middle school years, I was bullied and I also bullied a little girl. I was afraid of the popular girls, and I didn't stand up for myself the way I should have. I learned not to speak as a young girl and it showed up during my elementary, middle school, and high school years. Things began to shift after my sister and I moved out of my Dad's house when my little brother and sister moved to New York. Let me back track. After my mother beat me, my sister and I went to school the next day. My sister told our science teacher what my mother did to me, and we were escorted out of class. We were taken down to the office, and we had to tell the authorities everything that happened. We were then taken to the hospital where I took pictures, and we met our social worker Ms. B. She was a beautiful white lady who had the sweetest spirit in the world. Nikki and I were now apart of the foster care system due to the physical abuse of our mother. We moved in with my father, next my uncle, and two other homes after that. We were "foster kids"; however, the social workers we met along the way were absolutely amazing! It was in a foster care agency called "C.V." that I found hope and a voice.

This agency was geared toward encouraging, uplifting, and pushing youth in foster care to be and do their best. I was exposed to the world outside of "my hood" because of the activities set before me. (1) I received counseling, (2) met other teenagers in the same predicament, (3) experienced committed adults who loved me beyond my situation, (4) and applied to college and was awarded several scholarships. In my journey as a ward of the state, I met two of the most beautiful souls one could ever meet: Ms. B. and Ms. Perez. Ms. B was a wise older woman who saw beyond the surface of her clients. She definitely had the gift of healing in her veins because she pulled out things in people that they didn't even realize were there. She loved my sister and me so well. She invited us into her family, and we became more than clients. We were encouraged and inspired to use our story as a healing tool. Ms. B helped us to see that pain doesn't define you, but it tells a story of great triumph and intense victory. It doesn't make you who you are; it only sets you on a path to be the woman you were destined to be. She loved us beyond our story and pain, and my heart, mind, and soul will forever be grateful to have crossed paths with such an amazing woman. I pray that one day I get to share in the healing of others. She allowed us to meet her children, and she even invited us to speak at an event. Her footprint in our lives aided us to be victorious despite the obstacles around us. Recently, I wrote on her Facebook wall:

Chaquana: Hey Ms. B.! I am writing a book, and I am currently a teacher! I just wanted to say thank you for everything you've done for us over the years! We love you!!

Ms. B: Chaquana Muhammad Townsend, this message touches me deeply. I have loved you and your sister since the first time that I saw you. Your strength, resilience, passion, and loyalty to each other and family was amazing to me. I am beyond proud of both of you for breaking cycles and choosing to heal. I love you...

Even at 30 years old, Ms. B's words still bring healing to me. I am writing this book because I am choosing to heal. I am choosing to expose and uncover the pain in order to see the light. Shame no longer has a hold on you when you share what the enemy may use to quiet you. Shame can no longer whisper lies in your ear when you surrender to the Lord and say, "I will no longer allow the past to define me!" Shame has to flee when you tell yourself, "God works everything for the good of those who love him and who are called according to His purpose (Romans 8:28). Shame has to flee! Thank you, Ms. B., for showing me that healing is a choice. I choose to heal today and until the day I see the Lord.

Ms. Perez showed me what patience, care, and acceptance look like. I honestly believe that when God makes people in his image, he creates them to reflect his personhood. Ms. Perez was one of the most compassionate souls I've ever met. She was kind, understanding, and genuinely concerned about the well-being of others. Anytime you were around her, you felt valued and important. She loved my sister and me with open arms and no judgement. I remember being welcomed into her home and treated to dinner. I remember being close to a mental breakdown at 21, and she was there with me. I remember her going with me to the hospital and loving me through it. She congratulated me on my accomplishments, and she always believed in me which encouraged me to believe in myself.

Let's go back to my mental breakdown at 21. I had just graduated from Tuskegee University with honors, and I had a flashback that took me back to a scary place. Looking back on the event, I realize trauma will cause you to behave and act in ways that are detrimental for your well-being for the sake of survival. I was fresh out of college and headed to grad school. I was struggling with doing an internship with an inner-city ministry again or staying in New York.

Nonetheless, my mother invited her "guy friend" over to

my sister's house for the evening. When they walked in, I had a blanket over me because I was half dressed. I turned to look at her friend, and my legs started to shake and I became increasingly nervous. I got up with the blanket wrapped around me and walked into my sister's room. My entire body was shaking at this point, and I remember being molested at 4 or 5 all over again. My mother's friend had the hands of the young man who touched me the first time. His body structure reminded me of that same young man, and I was afraid. I called my mother into the room and asked her to have him leave because I didn't know what was happening to me. She became furious and eventually they both left. My body was still in shock, so I called two close friends to help me work through what was happening. That's when my healing journey actually began; it was the summer of 2010 when I realized I needed serious counseling because I had never dealt with the trauma of my past.

Ms. B became involved, and I was taken to a hospital to get evaluated. After the hospital visit, the nightmares increased and I ended up contacting a friend who was a social worker. The nightmares kept me from sleeping, and I was tempted to self-harm to rid myself of the pain. I was encouraged to contact a sexual abuse hotline to speak with someone to help me work through the inner turmoil. I also visited a friend who helped me in processing my internal and oftentimes debilitating and shameful pain. The facing of the pain began when I was 21, but its effects has had tremendous effects on my view of God and men. Throughout the course of my life, I have seen victories, defeats, and lessons that have shaped me into a resilient but scarred woman.

Nonetheless, God is intentional! He used my breakdown to show me the **need** for healing. I was angry, hurt, and trying to connect with a God that I didn't fully trust. He wanted to heal my broken and wounded heart, but I had to face the pain first. Contrary to popular belief, putting scriptures on top of your pain without honestly giving it to God is not true healing. Face it, give it to God, and then allow him to heal you. It takes a lot of courage to hand up your innermost thoughts and feelings to someone you are afraid will not still love you after the truth is exposed. However, our God can be trusted and He provides healing when we believe in His promises. I am reminded of the woman who was bleeding for twelve years. She went to many different doctors and had spent all she had, but she knew and believed that her healing would come from the ultimate healer. Lord, help us to trust you in the same way.

Mark 5:27-29: When she heard about Jesus, she came up behind him in the crowd and touched his cloak, because she thought, "If I just touch his clothes, I will be healed." Immediately her bleeding stopped and she felt in her body that she was freed from her suffering.

CHRIST INTERVENES

As a freshman at Tuskegee University, I was insecure, longing for acceptance, and eager to find peace and fulfillment. Sex was never my go to or struggle. Even though I wasn't a virgin, I knew I didn't want to give my body away to be used or taken for granted any longer. I was tired of giving sex in hopes of being loved. I slept with four guys from age 14 to 16, and I did not enjoy sex because I was emotionally disengaged. I wanted to be cared for outside of the physical realm, and unfortunately, I never received that. How could I expect something from young men who didn't know who they were?

One of my main reasons for not engaging in sex was ironic yet wise: I was afraid to go to hell because of my sin. Where did I get that notion? One of my friends in high school invited me to church consistently. I accepted her offer because I was longing for some type of hope and fulfillment. One day, her pastor said these horrific words that scared the living daylights out of me: "If you keep having sex and living for yourself, you will go to hell!" I made a vow that day, at 16 years old in Brooklyn, NY, to remain abstinent until I was married! Fourteen years later at 30, I remained abstinent with a few close calls and mistakes along the way.

I met Jesus at the end of my freshman year at 18 years olds. Before then, the Lord began working on me while I was in high school. Number one, a preacher scared me into fearing hell. Number two, I told my African American Studies teacher that I was going to find a good church home when I went to Tuskegee. That was all of Jesus speaking through me because my heart was so far from the Lord. I was smart, but I was living for myself. However, there was an emptiness that I couldn't shake. I was filled with self-hatred and shame due to my own sin and the sin of others. Shame filled my bones due to the sexual and emotional abuse, and I was longing to experience real, genuine, faithful, and enduring love. The Lord knew why he brought me all the way to Tuskegee University from New York City, and as I look back on it, it brings me great joy!

My transformation and conversion to Christ started at Adams Hall when the Lord blessed me to meet two of the most amazing God-fearing young women I've ever met: K. and A. Williams. They were my RA's also known as resident assistants. They loved the mess out of Jesus! They were unashamed prayer warriors and lovers of the word of God. They held a bible study in the dorm that I came to hear and there. They also held prayer sometimes throughout the week. These girls love for God intrigued me and pushed me to ask questions about who God was. I was also introduced to C. O. Ministries. This ministry held bible studies on campus and offered a summer project for students to grow closer to Jesus.

I went to church with A. Williams, attended Bible study and

prayer, and I even prayed to receive Christ, but I knew my heart was changed. I was searching and longing for a transformation, but it wouldn't happen until the end of my freshman year. C. O. had a summer project coming up. It was at the end of the school year in 2007. My plan was to go to summer school and learn about Jesus on my own. Nevertheless, there was a tug on my heart to get to know Jesus at the summer project. The summer project was geared specifically towards helping college students grow in their walk with the Lord, and my soul craved that. The love I didn't receive from my parents and the young men I gave my body to was the love I so desperately wanted! Little did I know that I would receive ten times more than what I could ever think or imagine.

I called Ms. B. to ask for her opinion. She was a woman I deeply loved and respected, and she knew me well. These were my words to her: "Ms. B., I can learn about God on my own. I want to graduate early, so I think I should go to summer school." Her words were strong and spoke volumes to my soul as a freshman in college: "Quani, I know you are smart and you can graduate early, but if you hate yourself and you're miserable, your education won't mean anything." Those words stung, but I knew what she was actually saying: "Go to the summer project, so you can be introduced to Jesus." That was one of the best decisions I've ever made in my life. I decided to go and the first couple of days I heard the Gospel so loud and clear! I was separated from God because of my sin, and the only way that I could be brought back to him was through His son Jesus Christ. I knew my sin separated me from a holy and righteous God, and I wanted so badly to know the God who did that for me. Another thing that sold me on walking with Jesus was the love and joy I saw in His children. A. Williams and K.

had love and joy unspeakable! The Christians that were apart of C. O. had joy that I knew nothing of. They loved God and one another like it was natural. I saw the light of the world inside of those brothers and sisters, and I told myself internally: "Whatever they have, I want it!" I wanted a reason to live because my former life sucked because it was a life lived for myself.

The project started on May 30, 2007, and I became a believer on June 2, 2007, in Piedmont Park in Atlanta. The project was held at Emory University in Atlanta, and we shared rooms with participants and leaders. I so happened to have built a relationship with a young woman by the name of K. Snead. Prior to the project, I went on a retreat, and I asked her several questions about the Lord. I was so hungry to understand the word and who Jesus was that I asked K. several questions. Several months after that, we were on the same project together and I trusted her leadership. On June 2, 2007, we had "Evangelism Training" which took place on a Saturday. I knew I wasn't a Christian because I know myself, and when God does something in your heart, you will know it. The night before I heard the Gospel again and even went to my room and asked Jesus to come into my heart, but my heart was the same. As the leader spoke about sharing "your faith" with others, I knew he wasn't talking to me. I was uneasy as he spoke, and I contemplated how I would tell K. Snead I wasn't a Christian. So as an unbeliever, I started praying: "Lord, please don't let me go with Kwajera. Lord, please don't let me go with Kwajera." I knew she was going to ask me questions I didn't have the answer to. I was determined to tell her that I wasn't a Christian, but I wanted to walk with Jesus because I understood the Gospel.

God is so strategic because right after I prayed that prayer, a sweet brother announced, "Quani, you are going with K. Snead!" I was disappointed and relieved at the same time. I was going to tell her the truth as we drove to Piedmont Park in Atlanta. I remember the conversation like it happened a few seconds ago. Before I get into my transformation story, I want to say this: "Jesus has been the sweetest thing I have ever known literally." When I contemplated cutting, suicide, and walking away from Him over the years, He was faithful. I have literally seen Him pull me out of depression, suicidal thoughts, and decisions that could have altered the course of my life. This love story is real! The realest love I have ever known, and I will shout it to the mountain tops: "I have found a real love! A love that is with you no matter what the cost!" My soul has found my truest love: Jesus Christ.

As K. Snead and I headed to the park, I spilled the beans: "I am not a Christian, but I understand the Gospel. I understand that Jesus died on the cross for my sins, and the only way I can get to the Father is through Him. I want to be a Christian." K. Snead stated, "We can pray now or we can pray later." I wanted to pray right then and there. In that moment, I asked God to forgive me for my sins. I asked him to change me and help me to walk with him. I remember both of us crying, and I vividly remember feeling a weight being lifted from my shoulders. It was like Jesus took the weight of the world off of my shoulders, and I had joy and peace that only He could give. I was genuinely happy for the first time in my life, and I was beyond excited to tell the world.

I was discipled that summer, and I learned how to spend quality time with Jesus. I learned to write out prayers to Jesus, study His word, and share my testimony and faith. C. O. set the stage for me to be unashamed of the Gospel, and I was discipled by several women over the years. I went back to Tuskegee's campus on fire and ready to share my faith. I evangelized consistently, attended bible study, and fellowshipped with other believers. I led a bible study on campus and invested my time into advancing the kingdom of God. In the summer of 2009, I was asked to be a leader on the very same project I became saved on! I accepted the request; however, I heard of two other opportunities that involved ministering to inner-city youth. After praying, seeking counsel, and the summer project in Atlanta ultimately being cancelled, I spent my summer in Montgomery, Alabama, with an inner city ministry. Two years after I became a Christian, the Lord sent me back to the inner-city to minister to children who were just like me.

This inner city ministry taught me so many amazing things in the summer of 2009. One thing the Lord revealed to me that summer was my racist heart. I did not like Whites because of jealousy and inferiority. I believed they were better, and I was beneath them to the point that I deeply distrusted them. I had a Caucasian roommate that summer who desired to build a relationship with me, but my walls were up. My truth and core belief about was race dominated my thinking: "You are white, and I am black. You will never understand!" The dislike and inferiority I felt around Caucasians came from what I watched on television and experienced growing up in New York as a teen.

Due to the conditions of the inner-city, I saw brown and black as bad and white as good. The media didn't help my thinking at all. The black people on television were loud, ghetto, uneducated, poor, ratchet, and lazy, and the whites were well-spoken, educated, and of the elite class. I hated being black, and I hated the people who I believed caused me to feel this way. I was convicted of my sin to the point of confession, repentance, and living communion at the altar to be reconciled to my sister and the Lord. The Lord placed me with a white roommate that summer who I coveted because of her privilege in America. I did not treat her as a sister, and by the end of the summer, I had to come clean about my sin. It was hard, yet the Lord broke the shackles of my racism. I was able to be honest with her and cry before her. The Lord restored my view of myself and my Caucasian brothers and sisters that summer, and I am forever grateful.

I learned that I had a passion for teaching, dance, drama and poetry, and loving on children. I fell deeply in love with the Washington Park Community, and the people that reside there. [1][2]My role with this ministry was to invest deeply in the lives of young boys and girls who lived in the Washington Park Community. I was a liaison between this ministry and the public schools. I was over the elementary or lower school portion of the afterschool program. During the day, I visited schools to check on students, ate lunch, met teachers, and built solid relationships with school principals and personnel. I fell deeply in love with every parent, every student, every intern, and everything that had to do with serving this community! Some days were hard and there were times students were disrespectful and parent relationship weren't always the best. However, I was willing to give my all for the cause of the Gospel. Long days, sleepovers, one on ones, discipleship, and learning and growing closer to the Lord through the highs and lows made me excited to go to work everyday. Something happened to my spirit when I was around those children. There was joy unspeakable! The good days definitely outweighed the bad, and I knew I was on a mission and on assignment. I was making disciples, investing in the academic success of the students, and loving on their families as well.

I grew in several ways as I worked in this ministry. I learned to love hard, persevere, and forgive. One of the students I grew close to goes by the name of Rockstar JT. When I first met him, I hit it off with him! Then as the school year progressed, he grew less fond of me to say the least. Most of the middle and high school students didn't like my stern approach, so they bucked against my authority most of the time. He and his best friend happened to be the students who made my job much harder. I was mocked, disrespected, laughed at, talked about, and simply mistreated just for the fun of it. I still stood my ground, but it took a toll on me internally. As crazy as it sounds, I grew to dislike JT and his best friend to the point of hatred. There was unforgiveness in my heart, and the Lord convicted me of my sin when I was around the two of them. JT professed to be a believer, so I called him out on things that were contrary to the word of God. I was consistent; however, the Lord began to speak to me about my relationship with JT.

I heard God as clear as day! The Lord told me to love on him and his mother. The Lord also pushed me to ask for his forgiveness in how I treated him and love him like a little brother. It was hard! Here I was a grown woman called to love on a teenage boy who disrespected me for the fun of it. One afternoon, I walked up to JT and asked for his forgiveness for my actions and heart towards him and it felt like a block of ice melted between us. There was a deep love and connection for him and his mom that blossomed. I fell in love with that family, and that same love still exist today. Although we don't talk as much as we used to, there is no denying the genuineness of that relationship.

I worked with the inner-city ministry from 2009 until 2015. Not only did I learn to love and forgive, I learned that Jesus loves me more than I could ever know. Let me explain why this is so important: One day like many other days, I gave simple instructions to the students in the gym. I told them not to do something, and shortly after I gave that command, they did the very thing I told them not to do. I was appalled, angry, and pissed off to be frank! The Lord spoke to me so clearly in that situation that it resonated deeply in my spirit: I have to remind you of my truth all of the time because you forget just like children forget to listen to the rules. That truth stuck with me and speaks to me today.

I was taught about the faithfulness of God as I served his kingdom. This amazing ministry was created with Washington Park as its target community. It was created to love, serve, save, uplift, and restore what sin left broken. This program was a God sent to the so called "least of these" according to societal beliefs and norms, and God loves the mess of my hood!! Yes, I am a proud resident of the Westside, and I don't plan on leaving unless my future husband decides to relocate. Please keep me here Jesus!! I love that God pursues his people and those that people deem unlovable. He died for the unrighteous which we all are no matter what side of town we live on. I am forever grateful for my time there, and it will forever have a place in my heart.

However, around 2015, the Lord began to burden my heart for the school system. As I visited elementary and middle schools, I met amazing, dedicated, and passionate teachers in the public and private school arena. I met teachers who loved their children, knew their needs, and paired up with the afterschool programs to aid in a child's success. I particularly grew a burden for African American males due to the countless cases of police brutality, and the disheartening mistreatment of black men and boys in society. It literally broke my heart and brought me to a place of confession and repentance.

I too struggled with loving the black man after countless acts of abuse and betrayal. I too held bitterness in my heart, and the Lord softened it after the two horrific cases of Trayvon Martin and Michael Brown. I was completely devastated that jail time wasn't given to any of the men who killed these young men. It crushed me, and I was determined to deeply love and cherish the black man and boy. I knew I wanted to teach by the end of 2015 due to several confirmations. On more than one occasion, I was told, "You should be a teacher." "Have you ever considered teaching?" One of my brothers in the faith called me a teacher. I knew the Lord was speaking to me, so I applied to Auburn University to get a Master's in English Education, and by the grace of God, I got in!!

Graduate school at Auburn was absolutely amazing! I met some of the dopest teachers and dedicated students. Three years later, I am still looking to finish my degree after taking a break due to teaching. Nonetheless, I learned how to teach through novels, how to relate to students from different backgrounds, and how to effectively teach and encourage reading in and out of school. My learning at Auburn and my experiences with the inner-city ministry equipped me to take my first teaching job in August 2016 at one of my favorite places to teach: a public, middle school on the Westside.

Due to my constant and consistent visits to the school, I was able to get hired through relationship building. It is utterly amazing how God strategically sets things up and hears the prayers of His people. I remember specifically praying to teach to a class of all boys, and the Lord gave me exactly what I asked for. I wanted to teach at that school in particular because of the relationships and connections I had formed with some of the teachers. Little did I know, God was going to use it for my professional and personal growth and spiritual maturity.

SAME-SEX ATTRACTION

I have a motto that I live by in any work environment: "Be the best, work the hardest, and be the most passionate worker on the job. Lastly, love others even if it cost you everything." In any professional job I've worked, I have been passionate, one of the best, and worked my butt off even when I wanted to quit. One thing I observed about my dad was his work ethic. He worked hard when he worked, and he rested well when it was time to rest. This motto keeps you progressing and moving along in your career field, but it can have reverse effects that can cause burnout. As a believer my motto should come with these extra words: "Whatever you do, work at it with all your heart, as working for the Lord, not for human masters (Colossians 3:23)."

The crazy thing about my personality is this: Around unbelievers may aim is to be a light and stand out like I am supposed to, and that is what I do. I don't work to show my unbelieving how hard of a worker I am. I work from a place of this is what God can do when you surrender your life to Him. There is still an aspect of fear, but it is a healthy fear because I know my boss needs Jesus. However, in Christian settings, I tend to do the opposite. I want to prove to my boss that I am worth the hire like I try to prove to the Lord I am worth loving. Neither my bosses nor the Lord want me to kill myself mentally and physically to prove my worth, but I feel the need to earn their approval.

With my first teaching job, and I can honestly say this in confidence: I taught with all of my heart! Many days were hard; I dealt with disrespect and saw things that were disheartening; however, it was a mission field for me. I taught 7th and 8th grade English Language Arts. I knew every student's name, and I knew many of my kid's stories. I got to know them, and they trusted me. Some days they tried to buck against my authority, but I spent many mornings and afternoons talking to students, stopping by homes, and calling parents and students just to connect with them outside of school hours.

I loved teaching English! We learned so much history about minority groups, read extremely interesting stories, and my students did an excellent job on presenting their book projects! They were extremely funny, and I spent a lot of time laughing in between teaching. As I taught them, I asked personal questions and checked on them as well. I got to know students outside of my classes because I genuinely loved the brilliance and beauty this school had to offer. I was introduced to more students through teaching dance and helping with the after school program. My pod or team members became my family! We laughed, joked, and came up with strategic ways to teach our students. We saw our scores grow due to hard work, accountability, and a sincere commitment to the students we taught. Our students felt safe with us, and even when the days were hard, I knew they would come back around and apologize for misbehavior or misconduct.

Let me be honest: I loved working with the girls, but there was something that caused me great joy working with African American boys. I had minor behavior problems, and I grew close to many students both girls and boys. Nonetheless, I made it my goal to treat those black boys like Kings literally. Why did I do that? They get enough hate, criticism, and judgement. I taught around you Kings who were in gangs, held guns, robbed people, and fought for respect. Nonetheless, I saw Jesus. I saw young men who were smart, creative, passionate, and fighting to make sense of the world around them. I taught through that lens. I saw young girls longing for acceptance and fighting to love who they were. I understood what they were up against because I lived through the same thing at their age.

I longed for acceptance and approval from my family and peers. I longed to have my voice matter, and I wasn't going to add to their distress. Now, don't get me wrong: There were days I was pissed off by the lack of respect and laziness, and they heard it from me! I was that teacher to love on you and call you out for your laziness. I did not believe they were incapable of learning; I believed they needed to be challenged and held to a high standard. I was a fresh new teacher, so I am sure I made mistakes; moreover, we had a great time in class. We read poetry, and they wrote poetry. My kids were amazed by the cases of police brutality and the books we read! They began to love reading because their teacher cared about what she taught. Some days were hard, but they were all worth it.

Every teacher has a few favorites, and every teacher has that one kid that melts your heart away. The funny thing is this particular kid wasn't my student, but I so happened to cover his teacher's classroom and we met. I was calling the roll, and I called a student's name that wasn't there. Pickett responded with information on the student, smiled at me, and said: "I heard you were the nice teacher." I was sold! We made a small connection that day, and I continued to build a relationship with him throughout the year.

Pickett is probably one of the strongest leaders I have seen at his age. He stood up for students who were being picked on or taken advantage of. If he did something, people followed, and he protected the ones he loved and considered loyal. I called him King not Pickett for a reason. I told him over and over again: "You are a dynamic leader. You care about people, and people love to follow you. Use your leadership in good ways." I asked him about his future goals, encouraged him to do well in school, and talked to him about the Lord. He was receptive and always checked on me during the day. He gave me so much hope. God can make beauty from hard situations. His life wasn't easy, but he continued to persevere. I called his home several times to check on him. I stopped by his house to meet his mom and form a connection. It was a privilege to know a young King who was flawed, but yet so loved by the Lord.

The Lord used Pickett to show me a valuable lesson: "When students know you love them, they will do anything to protect you." Pickett knew my love for him was genuine, so in return, he protected me from students. I know this sounds weird, so let me clear up any confusion. He would walk into my class randomly and say: "Are you good Ms. Townsend?"

"If anybody messes with you, just let me know." One day I was outside with students and walked up and said: "Ya'll better know be messing with my favorite teacher. You good Ms. Townsend?"

He always gave me hugs and made my day pleasant. The days I had to call him out on his mess wasn't easy, but he listened because he knew I loved him. Pickett showed me that the way a teacher treats a student can determine that student's actions and perceptions. He was excited to tell me about his gains in math, and he was sent to my room once because I was one of the teachers he trusted. There were several other students who confided in me and loved on me as a first year teacher at Southlawn, and it blessed my soul. One experience with a female student, caused me to see that I am no different from my students. The only difference is age, and the working power of the Holy Spirit.

One of my 8th graders was exposed on Facebook performing an indecent act. She didn't know she was being recorded, so when it was exposed, she tried to commit suicide. She was embarrassed because of the comments of her peers. One day she came into my room to talk to me about the situation. I was in my late 20's, and I had never done what she did, but I knew what embarrassment felt like. More than that, I knew what shame felt like. I knew what it felt like to feel nasty or dirty because of an act you participated in. She was a gorgeous girl who liked the attention of boys. Most girls and women want to be wanted and found attractive, so I understood where she was coming from. She explained to me what had happened, and my question to her was: "What made you say yes to him?" Her words hit me like a ton of bricks: "I wanted to please him."

At that moment, I could have rebuked her and told her she was crazy, but I didn't. I told her I get it. My words were simple: "Girl, I am no different from you. One of my greatest sins and struggles is people-pleasing. I am afraid to tell people no because I am afraid of being rejected." I told her that what she did wasn't the wisest, but this can be a lesson for future references. I was able to connect with my students because I got to know the other side of them, and I was okay with it. I taught the whole student, not just the "academic" side of them, and I was grateful for the opportunity. Overall, the school taught me to connect holistically, and I am forever grateful. When I visit there now, I still know students because of the relationships I formed while I was there. Some of my former students still reach out to me because the bond we formed was genuine. That type of teaching kept me going everyday. I can honestly say that the discomfort didn't come from the kids; it came from my own sin and that of another.

So here's the part of the story I am trembling to tell because it shows a deep failure in my life. The Lord humbled me while I was at this school very quickly, and it was one of the darkest and most painful seasons of my life. I had teacher joy for sure because children have a way of making the sunshine when it's dark all around you. That's not cliche at all. When things were hard at the inner-city ministry and in the classroom, kids had a way of helping me to remember why I was there in the first place. They can be the calm to the storm. As a single woman, I know

God has called me to work with youth. I literally go to bed thinking about my students/scholars. My heart beats for them because at the end of the day, God calls me to make disciples and to love selflessly even when I don't like them in the moment. Let's go back to the original story. I knew I was going into a dark place. Before I was hired at this public school, I talked to a former teacher who warned me of the darkness. He was a strong believer, and I trusted his judgment. I assumed that the craziness would come from the children, but it came from the adults.

As a young attractive teacher, I found MPS to be toxic and detrimental. Most men and women in their 20's, 30's, and 40's are looking to find love or a romantic connection. I had no clue that men and women preyed on new teachers. I had no idea that people slept with people they worked with. I was completely naive to that part of the working world. When I got to my first teaching job, I was asked out the first week of school. I along with another young teacher became targets. I had turned down both married and single men while there because I knew where that would end.

However, if I am honest, I was vulnerable for a couple of reasons: "I had recently broken up with someone who I can honestly say I loved." I cut it off for immaturity reasons, and it just wasn't the right season for us. I needed to grow and so did he. Ironically, we are really good friends now, but that's for a later time. I still had very strong feelings for him, and we communicated off and on, yet the Lord had work to do. I was angry, bitter, and completely done with men. He wasn't the only man I dated, but I was so tired of being disappointed in men. I struggled with same-sex attraction as a Christian woman internally, but no one ever tempted me until I met her.

I have met beautiful women, but this girl was gorgeous! The enemy knows your weaknesses for sure. Sadly, she was my type: She looked like a man, but she was drop dead gorgeous. I convinced myself that a woman wouldn't hurt me like all the other men from my present and past, so this was safer. What a lie! I never suspected anything until things started to happen. The one thing I can say about the Lord that reigns true: "He will warn you when something isn't right." We as Christians must listen to the sound of His voice and obey immediately.

When I got to school, I met some of my coworkers, and I went about my business. I was not looking for anyone or seeking anything out honestly. This particular coworker added me on Facebook, and my first initial thought came directly from the Holy Spirit: "She either likes you, or she is observing your life because she sees your light." I had never spoken to this woman or interacted with her, so I knew she was watching for a reason. Warning number one. Naively, I walked up to her and asked her about her teaching career. I just wanted to be friendly because she was my Facebook friend. That interaction was extremely awkward. She didn't look me in the eyes, and she seemed very nervous. It confused me, so I just assumed she was an awkward person.

The next thing happened: She posted a status on Facebook about church options, and I was so excited to invite her to my church! I had no idea I was being baited in. People, including me, commented on her status. I knew without the shadow of a doubt she would be at church on Sunday. On Sunday, when I looked up, she was there. Not only was she there but so was my ex. They both told me they knew each other, and I just thought it was a coincidence. I thought nothing of it. Little did I know that she had gone through my pictures on Facebook and inboxed my ex-boyfriend just to ask questions about my personality. I sat next to her in church, hugged her, and couldn't believe she came to church. I felt like a missionary at school. My coworker, who happened to be gay, wanted to give God a try.

I am reminded of the scripture in James (1:13-15): "When tempted, no one should say, "God is tempting me." For God cannot be tempted by evil, nor does he tempt anyone; but each person is tempted when they are dragged away by their own evil desire and enticed. Then, after desire has conceived, it gives birth to sin; and sin, when it is full-grown, gives birth to death." I sensed an attraction from her, but I didn't want to jump the gun. However, once she confessed to having an attraction to me, I told her thank you for telling me. Then, I talked to her about the love of Jesus. I thought and actually believed I was strong enough to never give into the temptation of same-sex attraction, but I was wrong. I was in a vulnerable spot. I was hurt by men and utterly disappointed with "waiting on a man" to get himself together. I was angry, bitter, and completely discouraged, and Satan came to sift me like wheat (Luke 22:31-32). I told her that I too struggled with same-sex attraction, but my desire was to please Jesus and not myself.

Over the course of that school year, after be warned of backing away from her, I became emotionally involved. Nothing physical or romantic happened. However, just being around each other constantly and trying to be friends through conversations and text messages caused our hearts and emotions to become intertwined. I contemplated crossing over to the "otherside" because I was tired of waiting and God didn't seem to hear me. I wanted "my ex" and every other man who hurt me to see what they missed out on. She quenched my longing for affirmation, love, and acceptance. I liked the attention, and in the end, it cost me. I was convicted of the turmoil in my heart, so I told her the truth: "Yes, I am attracted to you and have strong feelings for you, but I am a Christian woman and I have to follow Jesus." The school year became hard due to the avoidance and conflict we were having. Words were exchanged, and we had to live with the reality of unmet desires.

That school year was great with my children; although, I had some behavior issues. Nonetheless, my relationship with her was so tense that I longed for a way of escape. I cared deeply for her and would even call it "love," but the jealous love of a heavenly Father continued to reel me in with His love and conviction. During that time, I lived with my pastor who happens to be one of my favorite people in the world! This man watched me cry my eyes out as I struggled with my attraction. He came to the school to visit me on more than one occasion. He talked to the young lady to encourage her as an image bearer in Christ, and most importantly, he called me out in love. His rebuke was hard, but extremely loving at the same time. He encouraged me to repent and change my mind about this young lady. He told me I was wrong, and that I would hurt the Lord deeply and the body of Christ if I gave into my sin. I felt like I was hit in the gut; however, his words along with the conviction of the Holy Spirit helped me on my journey to change my mind.

This sin had me bogged down, depressed, and contemplating if I should walk away from the faith or not. I was trying to justify why same-sex attraction was okay, but I could not back my sin up with scripture. It was clear that it was wrong, and I had to trust the Lord with the pain of unmet desires and continual disappointments. God's word was clear, and his wrath is for the man or woman who chooses to go after their on evil desires: *The wrath of God is being revealed from heaven against all the godlessness and wickedness of people, who suppress the truth by their wickedness, since what may be known about God is plain to them* (Romans 1:18-19). My coworker along with myself knew the truth, yet we suppressed the truth because of our own wickedness. As a witness for Christ, I not only defamed His name, but I hurt someone in the process. I should have never become her friend knowing my own struggle and hers. My heart and actions flirted with the idea, but I knew I had to turn to Christ.

It's crazy how Satan works because I knew I was brought to that particular school to minister to and teach young minds; nevertheless, I became distracted and wounded in the process. I had to face the reality that I was hurt and harbored unforgiveness toward one man in particular, and I was deeply dissatisfied with being alone. I never lost my teacher joy, but I lost my spiritual joy. I fought to come to church, and I wanted to believe that there was glory on the other side of this.

The Lord used Psalm 23 to help me to see His amazing love and hand on my life even when I wanted to give up and throw in the towel. I had people praying for me, encouraging me, and reminding me of who God was. Unfortunately, I hurt some friends in the process due to my isolation and internal battle; nonetheless, God restored those relationships. Psalm 23 helped me to see that the Lord was indeed with me as I battled my flesh, and the demonic forces I faced day in and day out. There was hostility and conflict, yet the Lord brought peace and cordiality to the situation. Although things were uncomfortable until the very last day of school, I was glad the Lord provided a way of escape and was beginning to restore my hope and joy in Him.

Listen to the words of God's servant David: "The Lord is my shepherd; I lack nothing. He makes me lie down in green pastures, he leads me beside quiet waters, he refreshes my soul. He guides me along the right paths for his name's sake. Even though I walk through the darkest valley, I will fear no evil, for you are with me; your rod and your staff, they comfort me. You prepare a table before me in the presence of my enemies. You anoint my head with oil; my cup overflows. Surely your goodness and love will follow me all the days of my life, and I will dwell in the house of the LORD forever (Psalm 23, NIV).

The Lord refreshed my soul even when I didn't deserve it. He gave me the strength and guidance to walk away from sin. He comforted me the many nights I cried out to Him when the pain became unbearable. He gave me an opportunity to repent and change my mind one more time, and for that, I am forever grateful. I didn't see joy on the other side; I couldn't see peace waiting for me, but He is a Father of good gifts. Although Satan almost had me, God came and snatched me! I am reminded of what Jesus said to Peter in Luke: "Simon, Simon, Satan has asked to sift all of you as wheat. But I have prayed for you, Simon, that your faith may not fail. And when you have turned back, strengthen your brothers (Luke 22:31-32)." Jesus was praying for me at Southlawn, and he continues to pray for me today. I am forever grateful that nothing or no one can snatch us out of the Father's hand (Romans 8:35-39).

REJECTION/PEOPLE PLEASING

Rejection feels like someone took a knife and lunged it into your gut. It feels like death if you allow it to. The older I get and the more in tune I become with myself, I see how my actions are a reflection of my thinking. After I graduated from Tuskegee University, I decided to pursue a Master's in Christian Counseling. My goal behind this endeavor was to grow in my understanding of how people operate based on their inner/core beliefs. In other words, I wanted to be better equipped to minister to the parents and children living in the Washington Park community. I knew the Lord was calling me to work with inner-city youth; moreover, I wanted to get prepared for it.

One thing I am learning about Jesus is this: "Whenever he prepares you for an assignment or task, he often uses that time to work deeply on you." As I pursued my Master's in Christian Counseling, I discovered some hard truths about myself that bleed into the fabric of my being and affect the way I view myself and others. These viewpoints turn into actions that take a mental, physical, and spiritual toll on my body. One of my core beliefs is this: "Something is inherently wrong with me, so in order to avoid rejection and exposure, I must please others no matter what it cost me and outperform everyone around me." The thought of this statement makes my heart ache literally, but this is how I live my life. I fear man more than I fear God:

Fear of man will prove to be a snare, but whoever trusts in the Lord is kept safe (Proverbs 29:25).

This belief developed when I was a young girl. Due to my parents' absence and continual mistreatment, once our relationship came to be, I internalized their behavior as a judgement on me. I always asked myself as a young girl: "Why doesn't my mother love me?" I often wondered if my appearance affected her love for me. I created a negative self-view and felt worthless because of the trauma I experienced sexually, physically, and mentally. Imagine being a young girl in high school searching for value and identity. Imagine waking up everyday wondering if your life matters. Self-help books became my remedy and reading for hours in order to escape my mental condition. I was a hard worker and used education as my source of value and significance. It's amazing how God used my time in grad school as a time of deep healing and restoration before I began working in inner-city ministry full-time.

As a full-time graduate student, I acted as a counselor and I was counseled as well. Those two years were some of the darkest and painful years of my life. It was there that I learned to forgive. I was deeply bothered by vulnerability and weakness. I didn't trust others too deeply, yet I longed to belong. I wanted significance, but I ached deeply. I remember crying loudly when I accepted the reality that my innocence was taken away from me as a young girl. I felt out of control every time a man had his way with me. Every touch took my voice away. I didn't know how to say no. I didn't know how to say stop. I grew to believe that being attractive and wanted was your asset as a woman. Attractiveness meant attention even if it was bad. I watched my mother and sister get attention, but it cost them. It cost them their peace, dignity, and self-worth. I wasn't any different from them because I bought into the lie too. I wanted men yet hated them at the same time. It was strange: Celibacy came at an early age for me because I knew I was tired of allowing my body to be used; however, I craved genuine attention, love, and respect. I learned to build friendships with young men at the age of 21 as a result of going through that program. The Lord used a couple young Kings to show me that not every man wants your body. I released the unforgiveness I carried for men for years and developed a better appreciation for them. They could be my brother and homie, and I wasn't in danger if I allowed them to get close. After years of uncertainty, I began a journey of healthy male relationships; even though, I had a long way to go.

I also had to face my disappointment with my mother and father. The compassion I have for my parents now is only something the Lord can give. I acknowledged their sin towards me, yet I understood the condition of their eternity. Let me explain: When a person is not connected to Jesus, they live to please their sinful man. Their actions are a direct result of the "god" they serve. You will either serve your flesh or your spirit. Listen to God's word on the two different natures: *Those who live according to the flesh have their minds set on what the flesh desires; but those who live in accordance with the Spirit have their minds set on what the Spirit desires. The mind governed by the flesh is death, but the mind governed by the Spirit is life and peace. The mind governed by the flesh is hostile to God; it does not submit to God's law, nor can it do so* (Romans 8:5-7). I was able to forgive my parents because I knew they were not controlled by the spirit of God. Their actions and mistreatment were wrong, but they were doing only what their nature produced.

Nonetheless, I acknowledged and faced the hurt and let it go. Crying and pushing through the pain and knowing that God cares for me in the midst of it, freed me tremendously. I couldn't hold them to a standard that was nonexistent for them. I had to release the pain in order to walk more freely as a woman. The Lord gave me a genuine love and respect for my parents; although, I disagree with their actions at times. I love my mother and my father, and I am no longer living as a victim of their neglect. It took a while, but from 21 to 23, I truly travelled down the path of forgiveness through intense counseling and prayer.

DADDY VOID

At 30 years old, the relationships that I treasure deeply are the ones I have with my dad and my pastor and friend Alonzo Brown. Although my relationship with my dad was rocky at times, it had the greatest impact on me. I honestly believe that your relationship with your earthly father has a profound effect on your view of your heavenly father. God designed that relationship to be a glimpse of His love for us; however, more times than not, our relationships with our fathers cause extreme trauma and damage. I can literally remember the very first moment I experienced great elation at the thought of seeing my dad and receiving a gift from him. I was four or five, and my sister and I were in New York. We met up with our dad, and he gave us matching sunflower dresses! I was so happy that my daddy gave me a sunflower dress because the image never left my mind. I couldn't wait to wear the dress that my daddy gave me since it proved I was thought about and special to him. That very moment created a joy and happiness that I don't remember experiencing again until my relationship with my dad was repaired years later.

After that pivotal moment, I don't remember interacting with my dad again until I was a couple of years older. He called one evening when my sister and I migrated to New Orleans, and I don't remember much of the conversation. I do remember the feeling I felt during and after the phone call. I felt uncared for, disregarded, and unloved. I was disappointed in my father. I didn't understand why he didn't see the need to stay connected to his children. That phone call was of no benefit because it clearly illustrated my father's disconnect with his children. At the age of 14 and 15, my sister and I lived with my dad after we were taken away from my mom. It was interesting to say the least because I learned some realities about my dad that caused great confusion and insecurities. My dad believed that women were to be completely submissive to men through cooking, cleaning, and service. I actually understood where he was coming from. The bible does call children to obey their father and mother (Ephesians 6:1). So if our father told us to cook and clean, that's what we had to do. However, he constantly reduced the woman's existence and role to serving a man. I never heard him mention the woman having her own identity outside of a man.

My sister and I constantly heard derogatory terms used about black women, and I felt less valuable than a man. My daddy made it clear that he was the man in charge, and we had to accept his authority even if it was exercised harshly. Instructions were given swiftly and authoritatively, and I remember being talked down to and yelled at frequently. My father called me stupid so much that I had to fight to believe that I wasn't. I vividly remember having a fit when a high school associate jokingly called me stupid. I went off and so did he because his words reminded me of a father who didn't shepherd my heart gently. I longed for affection and care, so I looked to other things to fill that void.

His treatment left me scarred and deeply afraid of any man

who was harsh or extremely authoritative. Men who were not gentle in their interactions with me were deemed unsafe and intimidating. I disliked aggression in men because it reminded me of the lack of care and emotional disregard my father showed in his interactions with my sister and me. I didn't want to be controlled or loved because I didn't make a mistake. I wanted to be loved because I was yours and you were mine. I longed for a father who treated me with kindness and celebrated my femininity, so there was a daddy void that I longed for someone to fill.

When I became a believer, I unconsciously viewed God as an authoritative Lord who wanted to punish me for my wrongdoing. I feared the Lord like I feared my father. Be good so you can be loved, grace and full acceptance is a concept I am just learning to grasp even after 11 years of walking with Jesus. It amazes me how your upbringing and small moments of pleasure or sin shape your entire outlook on life. The Lord had to deprogram my fear of men over the course of several years, and his work is still being perfected in me. I can genuinely interact with men, and the interactions are less difficult. However, there are still ways in which I allow myself to hold back or shrink around men who are in authority or authoritative. Submission and honoring a man comes easy to me because I was taught to reverence a man due to his leadership position. Although I haven't been perfect, I have learned to deeply honor and respect the position the Lord has put a man in despite the faulty view of inferiority and superiority that was ingrained in me.

My view of the Lord has drastically grown over the years. God's faithfulness to me has truly rocked my world!! The love that runs deep in my soul for the Lord comes from watching Him love and pursue me despite my mess. I do not understand why He loves me. I don't understand why His forgiveness is mine! I know without a shadow of a doubt that I belong to Him because His love never fails or runs out. He is good to me when I am up, and he is good to me when I am down. I know what it feels like to be loved deeply and wholly because God keeps rescuing me when my foot slips. Oh what a faithful father I have! The Lord has used my pastor Zo and many other men to show his great love and care for me.

The first time I interacted with Zo was as a freshman on Tuskegee University's campus. He was the most genuine person I had ever met. He was extremely kind, and he genuinely wanted to build a friendship with me as a campus minister. I honestly didn't have any discomfort or reservations about him. His gentleness allowed me to let my guard down and enjoy being around both Christian men and women. I remember telling him that he was the father that I wish I had. He was like a big brother, and he still is. He checked on me, encouraged me, and stayed consistent while I was a student at Tuskegee University, and we are still connected to this day.

I met him as a 17 year old freshman and over the years, he and his wife have seen my ups, my downs, and my comebacks. I have lived with him, and I actually feel apart of the family. If the Lord does allow me to get married, I want him to be apart of the ceremony. His leadership, covering, and encouragement over the years has kept me encouraged and steadfast when my heart wanted to do otherwise. I am grateful for his life, and his leadership over the years.

PERFORMANCE JUNKIE/I TEACH

I know with all of my heart that God has called me to teach African American and minority boys and girls. There is a joy and excitement that children bring me that I cannot explain. Their smiles, innocence, curiosity, honesty, and sinful nature intrigues, excites, and compels me to love in ways that I never could imagine! They are definitely my cup of tea, and my joy on this side of heaven. However, as a third year teacher (one year in public, and a year in a half in private), I had to figure out along the way that obedience and walking in your purpose God's way brings more joy than anything else. Teaching cannot be about "performance" or the "approval of man," but it must be about God's kingdom and purpose for the minds you are educating. Teaching became joyless when I took my eyes off of Jesus and placed it on "performance." Let's start at the beginning.

I remember when the Lord started to put a burden on my heart to teach. It began in 2015. As a parent and school liaison between the Montgomery Public School and an inner-city ministry, I watched amazing, dedicated, and competent public school teachers teach young minds. I witnessed excellent classroom management, stern conversations, potent organizational skills, and a genuine heart to educate disadvantaged children. On the flipside, I have also witnessed honest frustration, discouragement, disrespect, and a lack of care and concern for the minds of our students/children. As I went into Southlawn Middle School, Bellingrath, Carver High School, T.S. Morris, E.D. Nixon, and Montgomery Christian School, I began to be burdened with how to play a significant role in the life of boys and girls for long periods of time. Although I worked with children in an after-school program, I wanted more access to them. With prayer and several confirmations, I left Common Ground to pursue a career in teaching.

Whenever the Lord gives me an assignment or a yes, he will give me clear affirmations through His spirit, a lack of peace until I move, the wisdom of others, and the opening and closing of doors. As I visited T.S. Morris in particular, I absolutely loved the drive and dedication of the teachers! I was amazed by their performance and desire to work with me. One day I was working with the librarian, and she asked me a question: "Have you ever considered teaching? You are great with children." I looked at her and said, "I have. I am actually considering going back to school to get a degree in education." I knew that was confirmation from the Lord that my desire to go back to school to teach wasn't a coincidence. The next confirmation I received came from Mr. Brock, the headmaster of VCA. He addressed me as a teacher. I chuckled inside because I knew the Lord was tugging on my heart to resign from my full-time job and pursue the field of education. I stepped out on faith and decided to apply to Auburn University's English Education program, and I was accepted shortly after. I knew the Lord was telling me to go because He opened the door for me to pursue my degree.

I knew the Lord was calling me to teach in the public school. I had completely fallen in love with one public school, literally. I loved the children and staff I came in contact with. Moreover, I watched two dynamic teachers master the classroom. I knew one of the teachers knew the Lord based on her interaction with the students. She was dynamic, and her students seem to feel safe with her. As I walked the halls and observed, I saw the bad but I also saw good. I begged God for a job at Southlawn and due to my constant communication and interaction with the school, the Lord surprised me one day.

I decided to move back to Montgomery and commute back and forth or possibly transfer to AUM. My living situation didn't workout in Auburn, so I asked my pastor to me stay with him. He and his wife allowed me to live with them, and I started job hunting as soon as I moved in. I applied to different schools in the city, and one day, I ran into the current principal of Southlawn Middle School. An employee introduced me, and I stated that I was finishing my degree and was interested in teaching at his school. He encouraged me to come to see him after I receive my degree. A day or two after our initial conversation, I received a phone call from him inviting me to interview for an English position at the school. I was hired instantly, and I walked into the classroom the same week. I prepared an introduction lesson, but I did not know what to expect the first day. Teaching was natural for me. I loved Southlawn instantly because I spoke their language.

Let me explain: I love African American culture! I love the

music, fashion, creativity, and realness my people possess. I was once a child growing up in the hood, and as an adult, I knew I would live in the inner-city no matter what career I chose. I know, understand, and believe in inner-city kids period! I do not believe the lie that they are not as smart as other races. I am an inner-city kid who excelled in school and received several awards and scholarships to attend college. I had adults who poured into and told me I was great, and I believed them!! I brought that same tenacity and belief with me into the classroom, and I had a blast with my students as a first year teacher.

I was given 7th and 8th grade English to conquer. On top of that, I was a dance coach because of my love for dance. I learned how to execute lesson plans, teach standards, and manage children. Southlawn was definitely challenging, and I had to learn how to navigate tough situations. I was cursed out, pushed, and disrespected on several occasions, but I still held my ground. I taught passionately, contacted parents, stopped by houses, and encouraged my children to love their heritage. We read books and stories, listened to poetry, and learned a lot of words and techniques in order to get better in reading. I learned along the way as a new teacher, but I had joy doing it! Some classes were more challenging than others, and I disliked some of the extra duties that were put on us as teachers.

Nonetheless, I fought to be the best teacher I could be. I was punctual and did everything I was told. Although I wasn't perfect, I knew I wanted to be an example to my coworkers and students. I was the Lord's ambassador, and I knew I had to represent Him. I was committed to treating my students as Kings and Queens made in God's image, so when I messed up, I knew I had to make improvements.

The hardest thing besides my situation with my coworker (same-sex attracted coworker) was the failing/low test scores which was a reflection of a lack of accountability within the school system, and the mentality of the children. Although I loved my babies, their environments and mindsets reflected a lack of parenting, an ignorance of how great they were, and a commitment to a culture that dehumanizes them. Most of my children didn't know Jesus, but they were some of the sweetest, funniest, brilliant children I knew. Some of my students were extremely bright while others struggled in reading. Nonetheless, they met my standard, and some progressed throughout the year.

I was taken aback by the homosexuality flooding the halls of Southlawn. Most of the girls were gay or bisexual and although I struggled with it myself, I knew it was a tact of the enemy to keep their eyes off of Jesus and on their desires. Sex and gangs were rampant throughout the school, so I made sure I prayed for my children and shared Jesus with them. I was unashamed of the Lord, so I had many conversations about Jesus because He was the only hope I could offer them.

One situation sticks out in my mind. The Lord used this situation to show me how I am no different from the children I teach. The only reason why I am not gay or sleeping around is because I know what I am worth, and I know the pain and consequences of sin. When I want to give in, I think about the pain, consequences, and disaster that awaits me on the other side. When I get caught up, the Lord constantly brings me back to my senses because He is committed to me. I will call her Queen. One of my smartest students didn't come to school one day, and a student asked me, "Ms. Townsend, did you hear about Queen?" I said, "No, what happened?" The student informed me that she was caught on Facebook giving oral sex to a young man. I also learned that she tried to hurt herself as a result of being exposed. My heart was broken.

When she finally returned to school, she came to me and asked, "Ms. Townsend, did you hear what happened?" I looked at her and said, "You can tell me." She told me that she was hanging out with a guy she knew, and he asked her to perform oral sex. She liked him, but she didn't want to do it. She gave in; however, she did not know she was being recorded. I listened quietly, and I asked, "What made you do it?" She stated, "I wanted to please him." When those words came out, I felt conviction and sadness all at the same time. I told Queen, "You know what's funny: my biggest struggle as a Christian is pleasing people. I say yes when I really want to say no. I please people even if it cost me in the end. I have to ask God to help me every single day." We talked some more, and I encouraged her. That moment was pivotal for me because it proved that the only difference between myself and my student was I knew Jesus and happened to be several years older. Even with Jesus, I could be in the same circumstance. I still saw beauty in the midst of extreme chaos.

I decided to leave Southlawn due to the coworker conflict, and the Lord was clear about where I was going next. Anthony Brock, the founder of Valiant Cross Academy, approached me on different occasions about teaching. We stayed in touch while I attended Auburn and taught at Southlawn. He was such a huge encouragement to me and still is to this very day. I knew I had to leave Southlawn for mental health reasons, so I began praying about what was next. One day, I prayed and asked God to make it clear if He wanted me at Valiant Cross Academy. I prayed for specifics. I prayed that Mr. Brock would inbox me and make it clear that he wanted me to work for him. Shortly after that, Mr. Brock inboxed me and made it clear that he wanted me to work for him. God has a sense of humor!! I went up to the school a few times, and I signed a contract for my second year of teaching. I was so excited!!

V.C.A. has truly taught me the power of excellence, classroom management, and drive. I would not be the teacher I am today without the help of the Brock Brothers. The passion, drive, commitment, and love these men have for education and African American and minority boys amazes me. I have truly found a family and home in Montgomery. The Lord began giving me a deep burden and heart for African American boys after the shooting deaths of Trayvon Martin and Michael Brown. My heart and actions were geared toward making every brown boy or man feel like a King in my presence. I was overjoyed to work with African American boys and prove to them and the world that excellence was easily within their reach.

The trainings, accountability, high standards, school visits, coaching, and evaluations pushed me to be the best teacher that I could be. I have literally seen scholars reading scores improve drastically through analyzing data, strategic teaching and planning, data driven instruction, consistent classroom management, and strong dedication. I received the best training from the best leaders, and I am forever thankful. I know what it looks to produce excellence and push scholars/students to meet your expectations. However, it came with a cost. One of my greatest sin struggles is working wholeheartedly as unto man. I am a man-pleaser, and I live for the approval of others. I want to be the best and get everything right the first time, so the concept of grace is hard for me to receive and accept. Perfectionism looks good on the outside, but it can leave you emotionally, physically, and mentally exhausted.

My first year at VCA was excellent! I taught with all my heart, mind, and strength, and the test scores made that evident. Nonetheless, I was working long hours that cost me a lot of sleep. Some nights I would get 3, 4, or 5 hours of sleep due to my desire to read, memorize, and master everything. If I got six hours of sleep, I was doing really good on that particular night. Don't get me wrong: I don't need much sleep to function, and I do believe there are times when you have to sacrifice sleep on behalf of others; however, my excellence was turning into workaholism which was causing great anxiety and a lack of joy.

I had to spend less time with friends and the body of Christ in order to meet the standards of excellence. I loved teaching 6th, 7th, and 8th grade, but it required a lot. I am not a "cutting corners" person, so whatever is asked of me is completed no matter what it costs me. I would be at the school after 8, 9, and sometimes 10 o'clock getting things done. I would also arrive extremely early in order to master my craft. Honestly, I did the same thing at Southlawn, but I didn't stay as late since the school day was shorter. When I had to attend counseling in order to make it through the school year, I knew my anxiety was high. One day, I had to pray myself out of a panic attack at the thought of not getting all of my work done.

The workload was often heavy as with any school. When teachers bear the spiritual and academic portion of a scholar's life, we often spend more time working than being with our own friends and families. Working with a minimal amount of personal time caused me to be frustrated, sad, short, and mentally exhausted. If I am honest, I made performance and looking good my idol and it cost me. I often led out of intimidation and a lack of grace because I wanted to produce perfection for my bosses, a good evaluation at the end of the year, and a great reputation with visitors. People come and marvel at the product, but they don't see the work that goes into it. I spent several hours in counseling due to a fear of failure, fighting extreme anxiety, and wondering if I should call teaching quits. Of course every school deals with defiant children, so carrying that pain was apart of the job too.

In my first and second year, I had to fight for joy every single day. There were days I didn't want to go to work because I was fighting to believe that I was good enough. I lived to make a "proficient" or "excellent" on my evaluations that it became about "looking good" and "performance." I taught out of fear of making a mistake, so there were times when I led out of a lack of love. I felt pressure to perform, so I put that same pressure on my scholars. Although I had some really amazing days at VCA, I didn't know how to be Chaquana Townsend. I was tense and just wanted to dot every I and cross every T. I was fighting depression and whether or not I should leave teaching the first semester of my second year. I had just gone through a traumatic dating experience, and the pressure of work became too much for me.

I started praying, fasting, and seeking counsel on whether or not I should continue at VCA. Moreover, I missed working with young girls and boys and using writing and dance as an outlet. Teaching started to feel too heavy, and I began to feel convicted about making disciples and really knowing my scholars/students. There were families and scholars that I was extremely close to, but there were some I wanted to get to know. When I was at Southlawn, I taught dance and two grades, yet I literally knew all of my students outside of the classroom. I built such a strong relationship with them that behavior issues dissipated. I was no longer happy at VCA, and I knew God was calling me to leave.

I wrestled with God in prayer because I didn't want to leave. I went back and forth and tossed and turned most nights. I asked myself, "Why?" over and over. I told myself I could push through it, and I told myself to leave. I knew I hit my breaking point when I cried my eyes out one night the last month of school. I was tired of performing; I was tired of living to look good for "the outside world"; I was tired of being fearful of making a mistake. I couldn't see Jesus anymore; my eyes were on "performance." I was holding onto my sanity through prayer, fasting, and counsel, and due to hard circumstances personally, I was suicidal. It was no longer healthy to stay in a "performance" state of mind. I needed grace, freedom, and wholeness, so I obeyed the voice of the Lord and decided to leave.

When I told the Brock Brothers, they were so supportive and encouraged me as their sister in the Lord. They understood my struggle and loved me until the end. I talk to Anthony Brock on a regular basis, and they have said on more than one occasion, "Let us know if you need anything." I made a commitment to stay connected, and they have kept the door open. Mentally, I was in a bad head space, and I know the Lord has to do some work on me. I am going back to Southlawn because I felt connected deeply to my students. I absolutely love working with inner-city youth. I connect well with brokenness because I know I can be a light. The same drive and passion I brought to VCA will be brought to South-lawn. I am a better teacher and more aware woman due to my time at Valiant Cross Academy, and my life will never be the same.

IDENTITY/GRACE

My struggles at V.C.A., Southlawn, and in life in general come from the lack of understanding grace and identity. If I understood the amount of love, commitment, and forgiveness God bestowed upon me, I wouldn't live to be accepted by man. It is utterly amazing to me the connection and love I have for inner-city children because I am one of them. I thrive at Southlawn because I understand what it looks like and feels like to be in the wild fighting to survive. I know what it feels like to want a solid love only to get lust and addiction under the guise of love. I understand what it looks like to be considered "the bottom" when your heart, personality, and who you are as a person is beauty at its core. I am a broken woman, completely in need of a heart transplant and healing in so many areas. I have gone left when God said go right. I have denied Christ with my thoughts and actions, yet for some reason, he puts up with me.

After several years of walking with the Lord, I see the importance of having a solid family background and parents who walk with Jesus. Even at 30, I have to fight the lie that I am not enough. I literally have to affirm myself through prayer and God's word every single day. If I am not allowing God's word to be my comfort, sadness and disappointment will overtake me. I wasn't affirmed by my parents until I was much older. I didn't have a man telling me I am enough in and of myself. I was constantly torn down and literally treated as if my existence was beneath a man. I was brought up to believe that my physical features were the most important thing about me. As much as I love my dad, he exercised his authority to keep us in line. He taught me to be obedient especially to the opposite sex even if it was uncomfortable. Grace and kindness came later on in my life, but the damage had been done.

The thought that God loves me unconditionally is a new concept to me. Every single time I hear about what Jesus did, it makes me tear up. His love is overwhelming, and the most beautiful thing I have ever experienced in my life. I am his daughter, friend, and bride. When I try to use other things to fill my sadness and depression, he reminds me that he is all I need. I am valuable because thousands of years ago, he chose me before the foundation to be holy and blameless in his eyesight. He chose me to have a calling, a purpose, and an identity. I am his, and he is mine. He walks with me when life is sweet, and he walks with me when life is overwhelming. He is there when I hate who I am because I am carrying shame for what was done to me and what I did. He allows me to mess up, and he convicts and encourages me to look to him. When I think of purpose, identity, and grace, my mind first goes to Genesis 1:26-27: "Then God said, "Let us make mankind in our image, in our likeness, so that they may rule over the fish in the sea and the birds in the sky, over the livestock and all the wild animals, and over all the creatures that move along the ground."

I was made to look like Jesus and rule. I was made to reflect who he is . I can speak, create, think, and influence others because

I was created by a speaker, creator, thinker, and an influencer. I was made to be royalty; I was made to make beautiful things and be beautiful because God makes beauty. Another scripture that comes to mind is further down in Genesis 1: "God blessed them and said to them, "Be fruitful and increase in number; fill the earth and subdue it. Rule over the fish in the sea and the birds in the sky and over every living creature that moves on the ground." With this command, I am called to increase in number. I have a purpose as a Christian woman, and that purpose is to make disciples and reproduce young men and women that reflect Jesus. My life was made to show other people the beauty of God. I am his masterpiece created to do a specific task: "For we are God's handiwork, created in Christ Jesus to do good works, which God prepared in advance for us to do (Ephesians 2:10)." I was crafted by the maker with a purpose and for a purpose. I am only walking in his purpose for me. What an amazing God!

I was made by him and for him in order to show off his handiwork. My brother and sister, your light and life as a believer cannot be hidden: "You are the light of the world. A town built on a hill cannot be hidden. Neither do people light a lamp and put it under a bowl. Instead they put it on its stand, and it gives light to everyone in the house. In the same way, let your light shine before others, that they may see your good deeds and glorify your Father in heaven (Matthew 5:14-16). I wasn't made for myself or for the pleasures of this world; I was made to point God's creation right back to him. I am enough because God doesn't do half work. God looked upon his creation in Genesis, and he said it was good (Genesis 1:31). The thought that God looks upon me and smiles warms my heart ten times over. He loves me because it is who he is. He delights in his creation, and for that, my heart is glad. I've always wanted to be delighted in, and now, I am reassured that someone loves me for who I am. Grace frees me while fear traps me. Grace heals me while lies entangle me. I am free to be creative, outgoing, cheap, funny, and compassionate Chaquana because God made me that way. His grace says I don't have to work to be loved, forgiven, and accepted; I am already loved, forgiven, and accepted: "For it is by grace you have been saved, through faith--and this is not from yourselves, it is the gift of God--not by works, so that no one can boast (Ephesians 2:8-9)."

STRONG TOWER AT WASHINGTON PARK/ STEADY FIGHT

I am beyond blessed to be a part of the church I attended. Flatline Church at Chisolm is an extension of Strong Tower. I am deeply loved and in a way that I have never been loved by human beings. They are my family because to call my church my friends would be an insult and understatement. I have built solid relationships and friendships with strong believers who constantly and consistently push me towards the Lord. There is a sisterhood and brotherhood that extend beyond race, socioeconomic status, and marital status. We are connected and completely one as God's word indicates, " For even as the body is one and yet has many members, and all the members of the body, so also is Christ. For by one Spirit we were all baptized into one body, whether Jews or Greeks, whether slaves or free, and we were all made to drink of one Spirit" (1 Corinthians 12:12-13). I have been a member of Strong Tower at Washington Park since 2012, and I have had my extreme highs of walking with Jesus and extreme lows. It is at this church where I grew deeper in love with Jesus through the conviction of His word, His people, and through serving. My pastors in particular have stuck closer than a brother. My closest sisters have encouraged me when I was knocked down by the cares of life.

I can think back to 2015 when the Michael Brown verdict came out. I was living with my sister in Christ and best friend K. Hartzog.. The story of how we met is quite simple. We actually met in 2012, three years prior. She started coming to Strong Tower after I began going, and we introduced ourselves one Sunday morning. Somehow, through the grace of God, we hit it off and became friends. Eventually, after a year of living alone, she became my first roommate when I was ready to enjoy community and fellowship in my home. God knew what he was doing when she became my dear sister, friend, and roommate. Our personalities just clicked. We both loved Jesus like crazy. We both loved our church, and we loved serving and loving on others. She and I didn't make decisions apart from each other. We cooked for each other, and we served our neighbors well. We prayed for each other, encouraged each other, and cared for each other deeply. The closeness we shared was God-given, and I was so grateful for her friendship. We both felt strengthened and encouraged by the friendship because of our love for one another.

My favorite thing about living with her was her desire to love and serve others. She often cooked and served our neighbors selfishly. Her honesty with me was genuine and heartfelt. I knew the Lord used that time of living together to show me His kindness. We had countless talks when life was good and when life was hard. When we started dating and opening our home, I appreciated the accountability. Our pastor lived right next door, so nothing was hidden or kept away. We lived our lives out in the open, and I can honestly say that we enjoyed the fellowship of the saints and the community of Washington Park. When heartbreak and disappointment set in, we comforted one another and prayed that God would hear our cries for healing. One weekend in particular was hard for me. It was 2015, and I was working out at the downtown YMCA. I remember watching the uproar in Ferguson, Missouri, over the death of 18-year-old MIchael Brown. I saw burning buildings, people marching, and the pain and cries of a mother who had lost her son. I also saw Michael Brown's body lying in the street uncovered. I saw video footage of him taking a bag and shoving a store clerk as well.

As I watched this footage over and over, my heart became saddened and enraged. I kept asking myself these questions: "Why was he killed? Why didn't the officer just shot him in the legs? Did he have to die? Why is he being criminalized? Why are people so judgmental? Why did a mother have to lose her son?" I was so hurt and still healing from the Trayvon Martin verdict. I was crushed that the black man was so unloved, hated, and completely emasculated by society. Most importantly, I thought about his mother. I remember house sitting that weekend going into a new week, and I caught the footage of Michael Brown's mother, family, and friends waiting to see if officer Darren Wilson would be charged. When the verdict came out that he would be let go, the cries of this mother were heart-wrenching and deeply painful. She covered her face, and the roaring of disappointment escaped her beat up soul. I lost it! I wrapped myself in a cover and held on for dear life. My entire body ached, and I felt like I had lost a son or relative.

When I got to my home one day that week, I remember walking into the house and getting under the covers like once before. I just cried. I felt helpless. I didn't understand why an officer who knowingly killed a young man didn't get charged. K. Hartzog, who happened to be home, walked into my room with some water and just sat there with me. She didn't say any profound words or read the Bible to me. She was just with me, and the Lord used that to help me process my pain. Her friendship is something that I am grateful for and blessed to have. Now, I get to share in her matrimony and witness God's faithfulness to her. Through her highs and lows of dating, God blessed my friend with a life partner! Her love for God, His people, and her future husband convicts and encourages my soul. I praise God for my sister and friend.

I don't think there are words for how much my brothers and sisters in Christ have loved me through the good, the bad, and ugly times. If I could share a few stories, I can think of specific incidents where I was rescued, encouraged, and shielded by men who love me like I was their own. I will start with my pastor T. Jones and his wife. Number one, it has been an honor and privilege sitting under his leadership for the past 7 years. I have seen a remarkable picture of what it means to live for Christ and to make disciples of all nations. My pastor and his wife have sacrificed so much to shepherd the body of Christ, and I am forever thankful for their service and friendship. There is one area of my life that T. has shown up time and time again, and that is in my dating life. Not only that, he has encouraged me as a sister in the Lord to constantly fix my eyes on Jesus and not the things of this world. I can think back to when I first joined the church in 2012.

T. has always encouraged me to use my God-given gifts to glorify God. Anytime I wanted to serve in church by teaching dance or drama for the Christmas play or host a Mic Check night filled with rapping, dance, drama, and poetry, Terrence was always behind me 100%. He has also been very honest with me when my choices concerning the opposite sex lacked discernment and wisdom. In this area of my life, I have blindly believed the words of men and allowed my heart to go deeper than it should. T. has graciously rebuked me and sat down with men who desired a relationship with me, but their walks with God did not produce the necessary fruit. Recently, my pastor stepped in when a situation became out of my control and fear gripped me and the young women living with me. A guy whom I recently dated happened to be standing outside of my window one night after we had ended the relationship. I screamed and ran as fast as I could when I noticed him outside the window. My roommate called the police and my pastors were next on the list. T. picked up, and he came to my house as soon as he could. He drove around the house to see if he saw anything, but no one was there. Out of fear, my roommates and I spent the night at his house.

I was embarrassed, hurt, and heartbroken all over again, and Terrence never condemned me. He lovingly told me the truth and encouraged me when I wept over the disappointment and sin. Every time I dated a man, he knew it wouldn't work out, so he graciously gave me his words of wisdom and loved me when what he had predicted came to be. Although I felt hopeless and beat up all over again, T. reminded me of God's grace to me and his commitment to love me as a brother and pastor.

I can vividly remember two phone calls that consisted of heartbreak and a situation that sprung up out of nowhere. T was there and always helped me to see that it was God's way of showing me I needed to focus on Him and not on what I didn't have. For seven years, he has been committed to my spiritual growth through prayer, counseling, encouragement, and several meetings. When I struggled with my battle of same-sex attraction, he walked with me through that storm. I remember fighting internally with the desire to go to church because I contemplated loving Jesus or being gay. Terrence called me to make sure I was going and offered to pick me up. Throughout the years, through the good and bad, he never allowed me to slip through the cracks, and I am forever thankful!

There are so many couples and friends who have been there for me through the ups and downs of life that I am forever grateful for. I think of many other brothers and sisters in the faith that have prayed for me and encouraged me when life was difficult. Recently, I had a brother step into my life in ways that literally helped me through one of the most difficult times in my life. K. Adams and his wife, Mrs. Adams, walked me through my last semester at my old school.

K. Adams and I became extremely close through talks, encouragement, phone calls, text messages, and home visits. This brother encouraged me when I was struggling with leaving my job due to my struggle with performance and the grace of God. He gave me insight on relationships when I had to make a choice to walk away from someone who was unfaithful. When I was strug-gling with extreme anxiety to the point of walking away from the Lord and suicidal thoughts, K. Adams consistently called, texted, prayed for me, and even fasted on my behalf. Out of nowhere, a meeting was held with my counselor, pastor, and Keelan concern-ing my suicidal thoughts and what I knew God was telling me to do. God was telling me to move on from my job and pursue Him wholeheartedly with my life. I signed a paper for accountability purposes stating that I will not hurt myself and will commit to calling three people if I am struggling. I was completely blown away and grateful for this brother's willingness to love me in such a concrete way. I am grateful for the Adams and my Strong Tower family for loving me so well over the years.

Lastly, I want to thank the Brown family for literally being my homies, friends, and second family! Words won't do any just-ice to what they have been to me for so many years. I have known this family for 13 years, and I cannot imagine life without them. I met Zo on the campus of Tuskegee University as a freshman. With my abusive background with men, Zo was definitely differ-ent than any other man I encountered as a 17 year old. Most of the men I came in contact with were either abusive or out to get something from me, but Zo's genuine personality and love for God drew me to him. He was extremely gentle and kind, and he checked on me all the time after I became a new believer my first year of college. I remember telling him, "You're like the dad I wish I had." Zo and A. Brown have stayed in contact with me consist-ently over the years, and we have always stayed connected. When I went to an inner-city ministry as a 20 year old, Zo was working there. When I decided to join Strong Tower, Zo was the assistant pastor. I fell in love with this family and their beautiful children. I had the privilege of teaching their son for a year and a half at Valiant Cross Academy.

There have been countless phone calls, texts, and life on life that have taken place over the years. I lived with the Browns for a year before I purchased my own home, and it was indeed a blessing! My life is an openbook before them, and it's hard to stay away from them for an entire week! A week feels way too long because of the genuine connection we have. They have seen my prosper, and they have seen me flat on my face, yet they have loved me through it. If the Lord allows me to have a family, you better believe this family will be a part of my family. Their prayers, laughs, rebukes, and encouragement pushed me to Jesus in ways that I will never forget. When I didn't have the strength to fight, they fought with me and for me. When I wanted to throw in the towel and walk away from God, their prayers held me together. They have been the hands and feet of Jesus in my life, and I couldn't ask for better friends. They have shown up in my life day in and day out, and I would not be the woman I am today without them.

The most loving thing Zo has told me hurt deeply, but it opened my eyes very quickly, "You need to repent and turn to Jesus. Turn the other way Quani. If you continue on this way, you will hurt so many people who love you." It was hard hearing that from a man you love like a dad. What hurt worse was he was right. I was so angry with the Lord for not giving me a husband and saddened by my experiences with men that I was in complete rebellion. I decided to give women or one woman a try emotionally not knowing the dire consequences. When I was in that stage, Zo held my hand through it and I came out on the right side. I decided to say no to my flesh and yes to the cross. When I think of the Browns and all of my family at Strong Tower, I think of this verse, "I thank my God upon every remembrance of you" (*King James Version*, Philippians 1:3).

TRUSTING GOD/
DATING

Some of the hardest trials I have had to face and walk through have been in the area of dating. As I write this chapter, a part of me is ashamed, embarrassed, and contemplating whether or not I should lay it on out there. However, the Lord has come to set the captives free, and He has finally given me freedom in this area of my life. I am no longer ashamed of what I have done, but I do hope to encourage the feeble hearts of single women who feel broken beyond repair. Let me start from the beginning. I believe every symptom has its roots, and they go deep. Before I talk about my dating history, I will first talk about my warped view of sex, women, and men. This goes back to the age of four.

My first encounter with a young man was extremely in-appropriate, and even at the age of 4 or 5, I was aware of the wrongdoing. When my brother's friend asked to touch me in be-tween my legs, I knew he wasn't supposed to touch me in that area. However, out of fear, I gave in and gained a core belief that day: "Men like what girls have in the middle." In other words, I figured out quickly that sex was a way to get the attention and shallow affection of a man. Most of my damaging encounters with men came in the form of compliments and touches. Since my father was absent during my younger years, I yearned for my attention and affection. I was extremely naive, and many older boys took complete advantage of that. I remember carrying deep shame at the age of five and adopting the belief that I was a "hoe" because men couldn't keep their hands off of me.

I liked boys and had several crushes; however, Satan presented the opportunity to watch porn and experiment with a young lady. I remember the showing of body parts, dry humping, and playing with objects. My mind had been tainted by my first experience, and I didn't talk to an adult about these feelings. The desire to be wanted, loved, and cared for only intensified as I got older. The affirmation, acceptance, and love that every child longs for was left empty due to my parents lack thereof. Although my grandmother filled that void as a parent, my heart had already been damaged and left with a gaping hole that I longed for my parents to fill. I wanted to hear: "You're beautiful!" "You are enough no matter what the world says!" Nonetheless, I received disappointment after disappointment. Rejection after rejection from parents whom I still loved so deeply. Although God has restored those relationships, the damage had already been done. I can vividly remember fantasizing about my future life: "A beautiful child with no father around to take care of him or her." That was my dream as a young girl.

I am a firm believer in this saying, "Children will more than likely repeat or live out what they see." Now, let me clarify something: I have not repeated every mistake or behavior of my parents. By the grace of God, I look like my mother, but God has spared me from having any children out of wedlock and I have never been physically abused by a man. Nevertheless, the relationship patterns I have repeated point to a core belief and behavior I have witnessed firsthand. Since men have mentioned how cute I was and liked my shape, I believed physical beauty and sex were the keys to keeping a man's attention. My mother has always had a nice shape and over the years, I have seen so many men approach her simply because of her curves. They have gawked over her assets and attention and affection were freely given as a result. With those same assets (hips and all), I learned to hiddenly flaunt my figure. I knew I was shapely and what fit right so capturing the eyes of a man wasn't hard for me. Ironically, I grew tired of men only wanting me because I was shapely, and I became fearful of them.

My sexual fantasies were all in my head, and my back up plan was to be with a woman if loving a man didn't work out. My first sexual encounter came at 14 when I was frustrated with hearing my friends talk about their sexual encounters, so I decided to "get some." The first time I had sex I remember being emotionless. He was 7 years older, and I just wanted to experience "it." Sadly, as we laid together, this was the only thought that popped in my head, "He's wasting his time, and this is probably the only man who will ever want me." The self-hatred was real! I was so distraught over how my parents treated me and internalized the sexual abuse to the point that I believed I was worthless. I felt discarded, dirty, and not worthwhile, and most men found it easy to take advantage of that. I have been intimate with four men over the course of 30 years. I started having sex at 14, and I stopped at 16. Eventually, I started to become self aware and uneasy about my choices. After each encounter, I felt used and that feeling was unbearable. I contracted two curable sexually transmitted diseases, and I didn't want to keep giving my body away just to be hurt again.

Looking back on that time, I see how God used a friend from Brooklyn to open my eyes to my foolish behavior. One day like many before that, I went to church with her. Her pastor preached on the consequences of sexual intercourse outside of marriage, and it frightened me deeply. He said the sexually immoral person would spend eternity in hell, and I believed him! I was terrified of dying and going to hell, so I made a commitment to wait until I was married to have sex. Lastly, I wanted to wait for a man that really loved me if he existed, so I became completely celibate. I have stuck to that commitment; however, my naivety and the desire to be loved has produced its share of heartache and pain. Let's start with the first guy I dated after I began working for C.G.M.

This guy was actually from Africa, South Africa that is. How we met was strange and interesting to say the least. He heard about C.G.M. through Sho Baraka. Sho Baraka, a christian hip-hop artist, was doing a concert in South Africa, and he happened to be there. How crazy is that! He emailed the ministry, and A. Conley, my best friend and coworker, received the email. She sent the email to me since I worked directly with people who desired to be a part of the summer internship. We emailed back and forth and spoke on the phone once, and I received a Facebook request from him. I accepted it, and he made his intentions known through comments and eventually, we exchanged numbers.

If I am honest, he wasn't my type, but I liked the attention he was giving me. He was okay looking to me, so I said yes to getting to know him. I loved our conversations, and he seemed very mature and the Lord was always on his lips. He was about 12 years older than me, so his life experience surpassed mine.

He was honest about his previous marriage in which his wife was unfaithful. I inquired about the validity of this through one of his friends, and his story was accurate. He was a nice guy, but he didn't like the idea of my pastors being so involved from the beginning. He eventually fell on hard times and asked me to send him money, and I refused. My pastors saw a lot of red flags, and they didn't believe he was the one for me. After months of conversing and skyping, I had to make a decision. With the disapproval of my pastors and others, I really wanted to hear from the Lord on this matter. As He always does, God spoke clearly through a brother and friend E. Armster and Proverbs 1: "Wisdom shouts in the street, she lifts her voice in the square; at the head of the noisy *streets,* she cries out; at the entrance of the gates in the city she utters her sayings: "How long, O naive ones, will you love being simple-minded? And scoffers delight themselves in scoffing and fools hate knowledge? Turn to reproof, Behold, I will pour out my spirit on you; I will make my words known to you. Because I called and you refused, I stretched out my hand and no one paid attention; And you neglected all my counsel and did not want my reproof; I will also laugh at your calamity (*Updated New American Standard,* Proverbs 1:20-26).

The Lord had been speaking for some time now. He spoke

clearly through my pastor and other friends. He spoke through the nudging of the Holy Spirit, and he confirmed it through His word. His wisdom was crying out to me, and if I didn't listen, calamity would soon be my fate. A conversation with my brother led me to this scripture. E. Armster approached me at church one day, and he asked me about "my friend." I told him that I wasn't sure of what to do. My heart was already in Africa because the thought of being loved captivated me. He asked me if I ever read Proverbs 1, and my response was, "Of course! That is my favorite scripture. I use that scripture with the children at C.G.M. all the time." It was in that moment that conviction ripped through my entire body.

I left the church that day, sat on my couch, and read Proverbs 1, and I knew I had to end the relationship. God spoke so clear that I couldn't deny His voice. I emailed "my friend" and told him that I could no longer continue in this relationship, and I never looked back. That situation taught me a valuable lesson about godly counsel. God will speak through multiple sources to get the attention of His beloved.

There was another guy, before I met the guy who I can honestly say I loved. The guy before "him" was a christian rapper who liked me for some time, and I honestly wasn't interested whatsoever. He was younger than me by three or four years, and he simply wasn't my type. Honestly, every man I've dated looks different, but each one has a look or personality that intrigues me. Anyway, after breaking it off with the guy in Africa, my mind started to give "the christian rapper" a thought. He was young, but he was a believer. He was attractive, but not initially my go to. At that particular time in my life, I was 24 or 25. I dated the guy in Africa around the age of 23 or 24. This particular guy was three years younger, but he was cool. I decided to inbox and invite him to Mic Check (an open mic night). Prior to that, I had conversations about him with some of my friends and brothers, and they thought I was being too picky because I was ignoring his advances. So, I decided to see how he would respond to an invite to Mic Check. He readily accepted the invite, and we began talking on the phone. He expressed his interest again, and I was happy he did. If I am honest, he filled a void that existed after I broke it off with the previous guy. Once I got a taste of the dating world at 23/24, I liked the attention and comfort it gave me. Sadly, it has cost me many restless nights, heartbreak after heartbreak, and deep anger towards men.

He and I began talking on the phone frequently. I came to one of his shows, and he offered to take me out on a date and give me a gift. I was ecstatic because he was a really nice guy, and our conversations were centered on prayer and the Lord. However, I noticed he had a girlfriend prior to talking to me, so I went on her page just to read the comments under her pictures. She was indeed attractive, and I wondered if he still had feelings for her. I saw recent comments from him, and I was devastated. The date and gift he promised never happened, and I backed away completely. It hurt deeply because it confused me. He literally liked me two years prior to me even giving it a second thought. He showered me with compliments, and he was clear that he was interested. I was disappointed again, and several months later, I received a phone call from him. I was shocked and knew I wasn't going to be the one reaching out. He apologized and asked for my forgiveness, and we decided to treat each other as friends and brothers and sisters in the Lord. That was the most genuine and heartfelt apology I have ever received from a man before "he" came into the picture.

It's weird to talk about "him" because he is someone that I know loved me genuinely. The amount of love and respect we have for one another is real, yet attraction gets in the way of that. If I can be honest, I wish "he" could be my knight and shining armour. The one who God made to love Chaquana, but the standards and non-negotiables that are a top priority for me were missing. It blows my mind how someone can love you so deeply, yet miss the main ingredients that make a relationship last. The heart of this man is precious, but there are parts of him that brought on some of the deepest pain that I ever experienced. I remember being balled up in closet crying my eyes out after he hurt again. It's like opening up your heart again only for your heart to be stomped on. Although there are no hard feelings toward him, close friendship is not possible because of the emotional intimacy that was shared. We never touched or kissed. He gave me a peck on the lips once; however, our relationship was never physical. It is because of that reason that our bond is so tight. This relationship had the most ups and downs, yet the feelings of unforgiveness and anger have completely dissipated.

I met him when he was 17, and I was 20. There was no interest at that time; however, I thought he was attractive. When I would see him, I would get some butterflies in my stomach, but I brushed it off as mere attraction. Several years later, we ran into each at a lake house when I led the C.G.M. interns in 2015. I knew from the time I stepped out of that van, he was attracted to me. I could sense his gaze and admiration from afar. We knew each other because we had met several years prior to that. He sat near me, and he asked me was I married and we talked about singleness. He went wherever I went, and I knew he was interested. You know the funny thing about this story: "I knew from looking at him that he was immature and not ready to give me the maturity I needed." The Lord spoke some time after that and told me directly from the scriptures that he was not the one. I remember where I was sitting, what city I was in, and the scripture he gave me, yet I was hoping God got it wrong this time. My pastors warned me again and encouraged me in my fight to stay away from him. However, he came in and out of my life and each time I gave in. He and I dated off and on since 2015. There were times when we didn't talk to one another, and there were times when we were just friends.

Recently, he came back into my life after a terrible and traumatic dating experience that I will discuss later on. He was there; I knew he cared and still loved me. The same attraction was there, but it seemed to get stronger the more we connected and talked through things. I had to make a decision. Although he is one of the sweetest and most respectful men I have ever encountered, spiritually I know for sure he is not where he needs to be to pursue a godly woman. Our conversations rarely touch on the topic of Jesus unless I bring it up. He doesn't believe the Bible is 100% true, and the reading of the scriptures in his life is little to none unless I encourage it. He faithfully goes to church, and he is in constant fellowship with other believers; however, deep intimacy with God seems to be lacking. Discipleship, sharing his faith, and being on mission for God is not on his radar, and it hasn't been since I met him. Financially, he struggles and dates were few. As I write this, it hurts reading what I am actually putting on paper. Let me tell you why it hurts. Jesus is the best thing that has ever happened to me. He is the hope of my today, tomorrow, and my forever with Him. How can I say I love God, yet give my heart away to a man who doesn't make Jesus his everything? As cute and great as "he" is, if "he" is not sincerely plugged into Jesus, our relationship won't last. Jesus has to be the foundation not how we "feel" about each other because feelings fade. I had to learn to really trust God with this particular guy and ask Him to help me say no to the temptation of going back to someone who is clearly "not the one."

After "he" and I called it quits for the uptenth time, two months later I met "Q dawg." My best friend told me about "POF" or "Plenty of Fish." I created a profile a while back, but I decided to add some cute pictures to see if I could get some quality interest. Shortly after I changed up my pictures, I received several inboxes. Many of the men I ignored or simply and kindly declined their advances.

One evening while in bed, I got an inbox from a gentlemen who I thought was cute. I liked the conversation, so I showed my pastor who he was, and he knew him! My pastor said he seemed like a nice guy, so I decided to go on a date. We went to Lek's Railroad Thai, and we really had a great time. The conversation was nice, and afterwards, we went to the bookstore and had coffee!! As a nerd, avid reader, and teacher, the bookstore is like Disney World to me. We talked about my favorite book "The Autobiography of Malcolm X" amongst other things, so I was so happy! Before that took place, I created a vision board and put the things I was looking forward to for the new year, and a good man was one of them! I was blindsided and ready to move on from "him."

I told my pastors about him, and T. wanted to speak to him right from the beginning. I told "Q dawg" about my pastors and numbers were exchanged. My pastors saw me go through the pain of dating before, so they wanted to protect me from another cycle of disappointment. "Q dawg" was married previously, and he stated that his marriage didn't work because they couldn't get along. We frequently talked about the word and the Lord; however, I wasn't sure of a true conversion to Christ. Church attendance and submission to authority are top priorities on my list, yet his church attendance was limited.

We talked about marriage, and he even asked me to send him pictures of the engagement ring I wanted. He dated me every week, and the affection and connection were amazing! I loved the walks downtown, and when I was with him, I felt like the only woman in the room. His focus and attention were on me. However, there were some compromises I made that I was convicted of. We started kissing and touching. We decided to back away from kissing and then we would fall back into it. Honestly, my love language is physical touch, so I had to really ask the Lord for help in that area because the kisses were sweet and his affection made me feel safe. After a while, I started to feel convicted, so I decided to fast and pray and the Lord gave me this scripture: "Flee immorality. Every other sin that a man commits is outside the body, but the immoral man sins against his own body. Or do you not know that your body is a temple of the Holy Spirit who is in you, whom you have from God, and that you are not your own? For you have been bought with a price: therefore glorify God in your body" (*Updated New American Standard,* 1 Corinthians 6:18-20).

Above all else, I wanted to honor God with my body and I wanted His will to be done, so I fasted and sought Him for seven days, and my answer came during that week. I started to feel convicted and concerned about "Q dawgs" commitment to the local body of believers. Whenever I would discuss my pastors or the importance of community, he expressed his concern or disapproval of the intentionality and involvement of my community/pastors. Let me make something very clear. My pastors are my shepherds. They have been given the authority to shepherd my soul as their church member and sister in the Lord. As a single woman, they are my covering along with the Lord. If my covering is not okay with my dating choices and their concerns line up with scripture, I am obliged to obey them! The Bible is clear about the role of a shepherd: "Obey your leaders and submit to them, for they are keeping watch over your souls as those who will have to give an account. Let them do this with joy and not with groaning, for that would be of no advantage to you" (*English Standard Version*, Hebrews 13:17).

My pastors were not fond of his choice to avoid a real conversation with them, and their concerns were legitimate. I knew if I continued ignoring and dismissing their concerns, I would be with a man who didn't take church authority and submission seriously. If I were to get married to him and things got hard, who would we turn to if he didn't believe in biblical submission to church authority? At the end of the day, the body of Christ has my back until I said "I do." The week of my fast I had a very detailed dream. I knew this dream was from the Lord because when I woke up I felt concerned, and I remembered every detail of the dream. In this dream, a woman came to me and told me she knew "Q dawg." She told me that he came into her life and suddenly disappeared, and I knew from that conversation that he would do the same to me. Moreover, the woman in the dream seemed very familiar. Before the dream, he and I had an amazing date night, and it was hard not to enjoy the company of this sweet man. His charm was hard to resist. I posted several pictures on my instagram account, but I decided to post one to Facebook. He saw me put the picture up, and he was okay with it. Nonetheless, I decided to tag him in the picture since we were openly dating anyway. I had just gotten off the phone with him, and I could tell from my notifications that he removed the tag. I was confused and hurt, so I decided to ask about it.

He told me that he didn't want people to be in his business and that I should have asked. I was confused because he watched me put the picture up after we discussed engagement rings. We were supposed to go on a date that week, and he stopped responding to me. I knew something was off by his silence. I ran into him at the gym, and he was distant and cold. He said he wasn't ignoring me, and he asked me to remove the picture. I removed the picture, and he communicated that he wasn't in the mood to talk about anything. I gave him his space, and I told my roommate about the dream I had after I posted the picture. My roommate looked at me and said, "Somebody came to me about the picture you posted. She asked me if you knew anything about his past, and I told her I wasn't sure. I told her to come to you." My response was, "I had a dream somebody was going to come to me. This is crazy. God gave me that dream for a reason." My only and last questions was this: "Do I know her?" My roommate responded with a clear yes and stated that she had been in my home. I was so hurt and disappointed.

The young woman, friend, and sister in Christ called me and told me she knew "Q dawg" and that his character and actions were skeptical and concerning. She went so far as to say these alarming and eye opening words: "If you were to invite me to your wedding, and he was the groom, I wouldn't go." I needed to hear that. He was upset about a picture; he was clearly hiding something, and he was ignoring me. After I ran into him at the gym, I didn't hear from him for two months. I tried to see what I did wrong, and it didn't make sense to me that a grown man over 40 couldn't communicate what was wrong. I knew he was hiding something, and I didn't like feeling discarded and mistreated for something I was bewildered about. I knew that was God's way of telling me he wasn't the one and to move on.

I got a text after two months, and I politely told him "I have moved on." He asked for an apology for how he was treated which concerned me because I never mistreated him. Shortly after that I ran into him, he said that he didn't like people in his business and my pastors in our business was a concern for him. I politely listened and told him it was nice seeing him. I knew that was the end of any connection we had, and I was completely okay with that based on his actions.

Two months later, "Light skin" came into the picture. The pattern I am painting should be clear by now. Each time I broke it off with a guy, I didn't give myself time to heal or recuperate. I was on to the next two or three months later. I was eager to date and find "the one" not realizing that Jesus was the one I was really trying to get to. Sadly, it took multiple experiences and this one in particular to wake me up from my slumber. From 23/24 to 29/30, I have made poor choices in my selection of men out of naivety, fear of loneliness, discontentment, and a genuine desire to be loved and cared for.

This last guy was the push I needed to take a step back and evaluate my choices. I have seen fine men on television and in passing, but this man was absolutely gorgeous! He was my type from top to bottom, and I honestly believed he would be different. Nevertheless, the enemy knows our weaknesses, and he knows Chaquana's kryptonite is men. Recently, I was on Facebook, and I played a game that said this of my personality: "Chaquana is the ultimate true friend. Chaquana sticks by you through it all. Babies, teens, adults, and old folks adore her. Although she's an amazing "greatest friend ever" kind of woman, she's also incredibly sexy and alluring. Many men have been driven crazy from their addiction to her. And that is her only down side. When you're not with Chaquana, life just doesn't seem quite as good."

My down side has been my relationships with the opposite sex, and I have suffered tremendously in this area. The last guy was a surprise to me. I didn't see it coming, and I didn't see the pain that was coming my way shortly after. I had just gotten back from a beach trip with some friends, and I got a friend request from a guy who looked familiar. I saw him at Strong Tower a couple of years ago, but I was not interested and involved with "him" at the time. I knew when he added me that an inbox would come shortly there after.

Due to my constant interactions with men, I know when an interest arises. I am a good reader of body language and natural attraction. I have encountered men in my day to day routine who show interest, and it doesn't take me by surprise. Shortly thereafter, he messaged me and expressed interest. He wants to be friends and get to know me because he was impressed by my career choice and interest. We exchanged numbers, and things began to circulate from there. My pastors knew him among other brothers, and they liked him. I visited him in South Carolina, and he visited me in Montgomery. Things moved quickly, and we began dating shortly after.

I decided to fast and pray and felt God giving me a yes to go forward with the relationship. We read the word together, stay on the phone all night, and enjoy one another's company. I was quickly convinced this was from the Lord. I tell him that he needs to figure out if I am the one God has for him, so we don't waste each other's time. My pastors like him, and he meets my best friends in Memphis. Everybody is fond of him, and so am I until what is done in the dark comes to the light. When "light skin" approached me he admitted to having a son with a woman he dated off and on for 9 years. He told me about his struggle with pornography, masturbation, and women. He also told me that he was walking in obedience now and that his sexual sin was a thing of the past.

He respected my boundaries of waiting until marriage to have sex, but the time spent alone led to touching and kissing. There were times when that didn't happen at all, but I quickly came to see that he lacked self-control in that area. I would give in out of a desire to please and a desire to be intimate. We were both wrong, and I started to be convicted once again in this area. I remember telling him that I didn't want to touch because it displeased the Lord. We repented, cried, and backed away from it. His words and questions often went to sexual matters, and he seemed mesmerized by me. I am not innocent at all because I engaged in the conversations and made sure I looked attractive around him to keep his attention. We enjoyed several and consistent dates, trips, and time well-spent until he confessed his truth. Before I get to that truth, I picked up on something that concerned me: his lack of self-control and leadership, and his words about women. He was said, "If women threw it at me, I would take it." He then asked, "How do you feel about someone else coming into the "marriage bed?" I was shocked by his audacity and sexually saturated mind. Other things were said, and I cannot blame him for it because I allowed it.

One day in August, we attended the wedding of a young man I knew. It was at this wedding that he confessed to being unfaithful. He told me it happened in July after I left, and he was lonely. The young lady came on to him, and he gave in. He couldn't hold it in anymore, so he wanted to tell me. I later found out through my pastors that it happened twice, and he had done the same thing to the mother of his child several times. It hurt like hell, but I was still ready to love and forgive him if he got the help he needed. My heart started to drift away from him when I realized he knew what he was doing, yet he was unwilling to acknowledge his idolatry and sin.

I forgave him and continued to love him as a brother, but when I started to see that he didn't see the seriousness of his sin, I knew something was wrong. I gave him an ultimatum: Go back to South Carolina and get some help or get some help at Fisher's Farm in Montgomery. Fisher's Farm is an addiction program geared to help men make Christ their everything not their addiction. He didn't believe he had an issue that was an addiction. He admitted that since he had been a believer, he would go two to three months at a time without sexual intercourse and then fall back into it. Sex was his idol and not the almighty God, but he didn't believe it was. I knew I had to end it when we had a conversation about his habit. I told him that his sexual encounters were a lifestyle, and he had an addiction to sex. He looked me in my face and told me that he didn't have a problem, and he was victorious because he got back up every time he fell. My heart was deeply broken.

I remember bursting out in tears as I was driving one afternoon to attend a Zumba training. I remember fighting sadness, pain, and depression because I didn't understand why or how God could send me someone who couldn't stay faithful to me. I remember being completely embarrassed because I had to be honest with my pastor and closest friends about his problem. I knew I needed to end it, so I talked to my pastors again and they recommended I leave him alone. I blocked and deleted his number, blocked him on Facebook, and the things he left at my home were picked up. I deeply cared about him, but I knew God allowed this to happen to show me how committed and faithful he had been to me and will continue to be because he was my true husband.

One evening after he met with my pastors and it was clear that we needed to go our separate ways, I receive a missed call from him through an app we used to use to video chat. I missed his call and sent him a voicemail. I told him not to contact me and to trust the Lord with the process. At that point, I was heartbroken and I knew he needed serious help. Hope left me because he talked a good game spiritually and we even read the bible together, but his fruit did not match his words. When I decided to obey my shepherds and listen to God's leading, I knew I had to end the relationship. I heard God speak through the same scripture he used to speak to me about "him," but I ignored the voice of the Lord. I, once again, thought God had made a mistake. That same evening after I sent him that voicemail, I looked outside of my window and he was standing outside of my bedroom window looking at me. I screamed and ran out of my room to where my roommate was. I told her to quickly call the police and our pastors because I thought I saw "Light skin" outside the window.

We were both terrified at this point, so we hid in the hallway and waited on my pastor and the police to show up. My pastor drove around my home and didn't see anything. The police officer walked around and didn't see anything or anyone. I was confused, and I thought I was losing my mind. I saw a few missed calls from him, so I knew he found a way to contact me when he wasn't supposed to. Somehow, he figured out how to reach me even though his number was blocked. I unblocked his number to ask him if he was outside of the window. I called him several times, my pastor called him, and my roommate called him, but we received no answer. He finally picked up, and when I questioned him, he told me it wasn't him and that he had decided to go to Fisher's Farm to deal with his issues. He even went so far as to say, "Are you okay? Let me know if I need to come over there." My pastor was standing right next to me, and he knew dishonesty was coming from his lips. My naive self was still trying to believe it wasn't so!

Eventually, he confessed to my pastor because he was embarrassed that I responded in such a way. According to him, he had no intentions of scaring or harming me; he simply missed me. That night, my roommates and I spent the night at my pastor's house where I tossed and turned all night. I was embarrassed, hurt, and ashamed that I had attracted such an unstable man, and my pastor, his wife, and my roommates had to witness it. My nights after that were hard, and I remember trying to keep my cries low, so my roommates couldn't hear me weep. Another broken heart, another disappointment, and I was the blame. I became extremely depressed, suicidal, and heavy. I had to be an excellent teacher while battling depression. I had to consider pure joy when I didn't believe Jesus was enough to give me everything I need. I contemplated not going to church and spending some time being angry with God since He disappointed me once again.

Then God showed up! I decided to keep going to church and one morning, Sunday school blessed me. We were talking about trials and suffering, and Zo and F. Turner dropped some nuggets. Zo mentioned the story of Joseph, and he stated that God knew

Joseph was alive and would use him to help his brothers who had done evil to him. He went on to say that God could tell us why things happen, but he uses it to bring about His purpose for His glory. I knew that God wanted Chaquana to see that a mere human being wasn't capable of loving me the way I always desired to be loved. He was the only one that can and will fill the void of loneliness, disappointment, and shame. Every time I fell on my face, he was there. Every time I asked him to show me if I should continue in this relationship or that relationship, he made it clear that He was the most faithful, loving, and consistent God. It finally hit me that Jesus is truly the most solid and loving being that loves me recklessly because He has protected me from every single man that wasn't for me! I received some battle wounds, but I came out stronger and wiser than before.

A dear brother stated that sometimes God allows people in the body of Christ to go through things to show others what perseverance looks like. During that difficult time, K. Adams and I became close. He knew about my depression, deep sadness, and suicidal ideations. That brother called to check on me consistently, texted me, and prayed me through my last semester at Valiant Cross. The break up with "Light skin," and the desire to perform was killing me emotionally and spiritually to the point of praying for the desire not to just end it all. I was just tired, but the prayers of God's people, His word, and the local church encouraged me to keep fighting the good fight of faith. The days following that got easier. The Lord literally gave me strength, joy, and peace like a river!! I can't explain how I made it out of that dark place, but what I can say is, "I knew the Lord wanted me to be free from using things and people as a source of comfort and run to Him." I started to go to counseling and work through the hurt and betrayal. I ran to the Lord when I was lonely and confessed my sin and shortcomings. Six months later, I can say confidently that I am okay. Some days I feels the hurt and pain, and many days I don't. Men have come into the picture after "Light skin" and by the grace of God, I said no. "He" came back into the picture and feelings started to arise, and I had to cut it off completely. I am okay and excited about my journey with the Lord because His love is so much sweeter after the trial.

During those nights of hidden cries and suicidal thoughts, I felt the love of Jesus. He was right there with me, encouraging me through His word and precious Holy Spirit. He gave me a greater desire to know, love, and serve Him, and I finally feel whole. Even though marriage is still a desire, I am okay if Jesus is the only husband I get to experience on this side of heaven because He has been the sweetest husband I've known. When I desire companionship, I run to Him and the amazing friends He has given me. God has shown me how faithful and kind He is, and now I can consider it pure joy when I face trials because I know who is facing the trial with me! He is! He is my rock, my safe place, my strong tower, and my help! I know He loves me, and I am convinced that He is jealous for Chaquana Monique Muhammad Townsend. I am a jewel and a King has to be able to handle a jewel. He is my rescuer and protector, and I am grateful for Him.

Single ladies, I know it is hard to believe that God has not forgotten you. I know it is hard to believe that He cares when you see people getting engaged, married, and pregnant right in front of your face. He is the God who sees, who knows, and who cares. He does not withhold any good thing from those who walk uprightly (*New American Standard,* Psalm 84:11). He wants you to believe and know that true contentment comes from Him and Him alone. The joy I feel is unreal! I am smiling more than I ever smiled, and I am so excited about working for the kingdom of God because Jesus is finally enough. His love has overtaken me! I am not pregnant! Thank you Lord! I am not suffering from a sexually transmitted disease. I am not in an unhappy relationship. I am whole and complete because I finally see who was there the whole time. If He did it for me, He can do it for you! I am living my dreams by teaching at a school I adore despite the fights and crooked system. I am publishing my first book and starting a business soon! God is faithful! I have always dreamed of being a writer and owning a business that empowers women. He is doing it because when I am doing His will, joy follows. Pursue Him and He will give you the desires of your heart (*New International Version*, Psalm 37:4).

Lastly, I want to acknowledge a woman who is indeed one of the biggest advocates, supporters, and best friends I could ask for. Kellee Ferguson is probably the only single woman that I have met with the healthiest and most honest approach to dating. She has taught me to love myself over the years. She has laughed at me when I did silly things and rebuked and encouraged me when I needed to hear hard truth. Most importantly, she has taught me many valuable lessons as a single woman. She has encouraged me to never settle! If that man does not have the non-negotiables you need and desire, leave him alone! She never judged me or belittled my feelings. She honestly and lovingly told me to own my truth.

I honestly don't know where I would be without such a solid and real friendship. I can be completely vulnerable and honest with her even when it hurts. She knows me very well and will call me out my dishonesty. She knows when I am hurting, and she knows when I am free. She is a woman that I admire for her courage, hard work, and willingness to go after what she wants. Her confidence and assurance in her beauty is convicting and encouraging. Thank you Kellee for helping me to see the beauty and strength I didn't know I had. You love me beyond my flaws, and I love being your friend and travel buddy. I know love is possible because you are a living example of what it means to never settle for less. I love you, and thank you for being my rock on earth during the good and the bad.

SUICIDE/HOPE

One of my biggest temptations on this side of heaven is the desire to "leave this earth" when life is overwhelming. The Lord's faithfulness has been an anchor for my soul, but there were several instances as a believer that I had completely lost hope. Most times the suicidal ideations came from shame, embarrassment, rejection, and deep fear. These times in my life I made a mistake and didn't believe I could be loved or cleansed from it. The notion or idea of suicide pushes a person to believe that God's truth, comfort, and love aren't enough in that moment. Life has its challenges and many ups and downs accompany it; however, the grace, love, and compassion of Jesus can help us in any situation. I am reminded of God's rescuing power in the book of Psalms. When we turn to God in the midst of our pain, He is a deliverer and healer:

"I sought the Lord, and he answered me;
he delivered me from all my fears.
Those who look to him are radiant;
their faces are never covered with shame.
This poor man called, and the Lord heard him;
he saved him out of all his troubles.
The angel of the Lord encamps around those who fear him,
and he delivers them (*New International Version*, Psalm 34).

In times of difficulty, especially in the case of suicide, we must seek the Lord and surround ourselves with people who love us and care about our well-being. Isolation should never be the go to when you are struggling emotionally. Our thoughts can lead us down paths that we should never travel. When I am struggling, I have had to learn to go spend the night with some friends. Being around others and confessing your struggles, protects you from yourself. When the truth is out, there is freedom and your brothers and sisters can pray for your healing: "Therefore confess your sins to each other and pray for each other so that you may be healed. The prayer of a righteous person is powerful and effective (*New International Version,* James 5:16).

There is something that happens when the people of God get together and pray! I can vividly remember going through difficult seasons and feeling the prayers of the righteous giving me the strength to go on. I knew there was no way I would have made it without dear brothers and sisters praying and fasting for me. My dear brother and sister, you are not alone in your struggle with depression, suicide, and hopelessness. Seek Him, counseling, and community and watch the days get a little easier. God promises to make all things new on the day of completion:

"Being confident of this, that he who began a good work in you will carry it on to completion until the day of Christ Jesus" (*New International Version*, Philippians 1:6).

ABOUT THE AUTHOR

Chaquana Monique Muhammad Townsend was born in Bronx, New York on October 15, 1988. She is the daughter of Linda Townsend and Abdus Ali (Robert Napper). She has three siblings on her mother's side, David, Benjamin, and Csniqua and 18 or more siblings on her father's side. Chaquana was raised by her grandmother from the time she was four until the age of thirteen in New Orleans, Louisiana. Her roots stem from both New York and New Orleans culture.

She moved back to New York at thirteen years of age and finished high school while there. The neglect of her parents, past abuse and disappointment, the death of her grandmother, and the fear of repeated a vicious cycle pushed Chaquana to pursue college at Tuskegee University. It was there that she found the hope of the gospel that completely and radically changed her life and perspective. After college, she pursued a Master's in Christian Counseling where she faced the pain and reality of her abuse and began the process of deep healing. She eventually moved to Montgomery where she worked for Common Ground Montgomery and joined Strong Tower at Washington Park. She currently lives in Washington Park and teaches 8th grade English at Southlawn Middle School. She dreams of one day owning her own business where she can use teaching, dance, ministry, and writing to glorify God. She is currently a member of Flatline Church at Chisolm, and she is an ESL teacher, dancer, and writer.

TO THE LOVER
OF MY SOUL

Words cannot describe what you mean to me. You are the one true husband and lover I have been waiting for my entire life! Thank you for choosing me before the foundation of the world to be yours and yours alone. Thank you for knowing me deeply and still sticking by my side. Your love is like no other. It holds me together when life is falling apart. It keeps me going when it makes more sense to give up. You have loved me with an indescribable love. A love that convicts. A love that encourages, and a love that has changed my entire being. Jesus, I am so grateful for a God who never fails!

This journey with you has been joyous, painful, exciting, scary, and life-giving. You have given me strength and courage that I did not have. You have rescued me from people and situations that were damaging to my soul. I want to love you forever and live to make you known. I pray that my nieces and nephews get to taste the goodness of your love. I pray that my sister, mother, father, and extended family members get to see the goodness of the Lord in the land of the living. Your love overflows and grips every part of my soul. Thank you for being mine, and I pray that my heart falls deeper and deeper in love with you. Lord, keep my eyes stayed on you. Hold me when I feel alone and the enemy tries to tell me lies. I love you Lord. Thank you for hearing my cries. May my legacy and impact be a reflection of what you have done and the power of the cross. My life belongs to you. I look forward to worshipping you forever!

DEAR BLACK MAN

When I think of you, I think of hope. I think of beauty in its purest form. I am so sorry that society sees you as an enemy. They have dehumanized you and torn apart your very essence. You are loved kings! You are amazing, and it is truly a privilege to know you. It is hard for many sisters to keep their eyes off such a beautiful sight. Sin has distorted God's plan for your life, but he is the master at perfecting what the world has disfigured. I will keep fighting for you and loving you even when your actions disappoint. You are still God's creation, made in His image for His glory, and I will treat you as such.

Black man, you are not a mistake or a menace to society. You are simply a product of a crooked and perverse world, and it is my prayer that you walk in the authority God has given you. Even though some of my experiences with you have been less than ideal, I refuse to label you as a curse because God made you uniquely. You are a gift to the world whether you believe it or not. God creates masterpiece kings, and I am sure you are a part of that greatness. So, I will pray for you, encourage you, and love on you every chance I get. You were made to shine. You were made to rule, and I pray that you one day you will see how amazing you truly are. May God protect you from the evil one and capture your heart with his love. Be kings!!!

DEAR BLACK WOMAN

Queens, you are the dopest beings on the face of the earth! Now, this is not a celebration of who's better because God made every race and ethnicity equally amazing; however, this is a celebration of the black woman-A woman who has endured so much, yet she still fights for joy and freedom when the world tries to trip her up. You are fierce! Beautiful is an understatement for the strength, courage, and divine essence you possess. You were made with a purpose, with a reason, and the world has always taken note of the black woman.

Sisters, let's use our giftings and beauty to reflect an amazing and glorious God. You are more than your hips, curves, and what God has given you to bless your mate if He so allows. You were made to point others to the goodness and magnificence of the creator, and I pray that you believe in the true beauty that He has given you. True beauty runs deeper than your outward appearance because it is a beauty that doesn't fade or run out. It is a quiet beauty that brings peace, satisfaction, joy, contentment, and depth to everyone around. It is a beauty that says no to evil but yes to God. Your beauty is undeniable, unshakable, and breathtaking because it came from an undeniable, unshakable, and breathtaking God. Be queens because God made you to rule!

DEAR SINGLE WOMEN

This book was birthed out of the pain of being single and hoping that the guy I was dating would be the one to numb the loneliness. I remember being on the phone with him after he confessed to being unfaithful telling him that I am going to start writing a book. This book was given life because the Lord knew He had a bigger purpose for my life, and it wasn't a ring from a man who couldn't stay faithful. Sis, I know what it feels like to believe something is wrong with you. I know what it feels like to live your entire life wanting to be loved, valued, and cared for only to receive disappointment after disappointment. I know what it feels like to be faithful to the Lord and still end up being alone. I know what it feels like to want something so bad and never get it.

Sisters, God has not forgotten about you because He is the only one who truly understands what it feels like to be alone. He was despised, rejected, and familiar with suffering. He was tempted just as we are, yet He was spotless because of who He is. He is the one who holds us together when we feel like giving up. He is the one who protects us when men come into the picture who are no good for us. He understands the lonely nights, the constant cries for help, and He will continue to meet us right where we are. Marriage is not the end all be all; Jesus is! God does not withhold any good thing from those who walk uprightly. He is good, and He is the one who gives us exactly what we need. His word stands true: "For your Maker is yourhusband-- the

LORD Almighty is his name-- the Holy One of Israel is your Redeemer; he is called the God of all the earth" (*New International Version*, Isaiah 54:5).

DEAR BLACK BOY
AND GIRL

You are our future hope and the leaders of tomorrow. Don't believe for one second that your life, opinion, and voice do not matter. You are a gift to your parents, teachers, family members, friends, and many others. Thank you for existing! Thank you for being you and allowing adults to take part in your amazing legacy. Cherish, respect, and love the adults around you who care for you more than you realize. You may not see it now, but their words of wisdom will make sense to you when you become an adult yourself. Use your influence and leadership to bring the world good and not harm.

We are rooting for you. It is you who make the world go round. It is you who give light to places that are dark. Your smile and life can bring joy to a place and a person because God created you to do such. I pray for the protection of your mind, heart, and soul. May God capture you with His love and keep you on the His path and not the path of the evil one. Shine Kings and Queens. Be great because the one who created you is great! You are truly a masterpiece and gift to a world that is looking for you to take center stage. The only way to continue to shine bright is to get your light from the one who shines brighter than anything else. He brings hope to the hopeless and light to the darkness. He is a father to the fatherless, and a husband to the one who is husbandless. Let Him be your guide because He will not lead you astray. May God keep you and help you to see that true love, acceptance, and hope come from Him. Be free, black boy and girl, to love a God that will never disappoint!

DEAR TEACHER/ LIFE CHANGER

I get it! I understand the sacrifice, time well spent, long days, and long nights. Brothers and sisters, your labor is NOT in vain. However, this letter has a flipside, and I really want you to listen: "Don't pour from an empty, overwhelmed, I just want to make others happy cup!" You are more than a teacher, and empty cups don't pour out. Those cups only get filled with more work, baggage, and weight. Let the Lord fill you help, so you are able to holistically, authentically, and righteously pour out! The battle is with the Lord, and your own heart, not with your students, parents, or administration. Give your students the filled up you, the content you, the you that believes in the help of a mighty God. Then, you teach with all your heart, mind, and soul!

Encourage your students/scholars to be themselves. Encourage them to be excellent because they were made by an excellent God. Encourage them to work hard rather than taking the easy way out and pray like crazy! Prayer will get you up in the morning and get you through the day. It will keep you teaching when you make up in your mind that teaching is for the birds. You are indeed a gift and life changer. Ask God to fill you with more of Him, so you can give His love to your students/scholars and those around. Lastly, don't neglect your own well-being or the well-being of your family. Your first mission is your home and then it's your classroom. Believe it or not, character and education go hand in hand. I pray that your character and legacy reflect excellence and integrity which infiltrates your classroom. Teacher and life changer, I am praying

for you. I pray that God will fill you to the brim, so your light can spill over to them (your students/scholars). God bless you!

TO KELLEE, AVA, KASEY, AND HEATHER (MY BEST FRIENDS)

I cannot imagine life without you guys. I am completely floored and grateful for the opportunity to do life with such amazing queens! You guys have shown me what it looks like to love even when it's uncomfortable. Thank you for every year of friendship and every labor of love given and shown. I heard a quote that says, "You are the company you keep!" Well, based on my company, a sister is winning!! Every last one of you are absolutely amazing. You are amazing friends, girlfriends, fiances, and wives. You are a clear example and picture of God's loving kindness toward me, and I am forever indebted to you. I pray that God gives you the desires of your heart and blesses you tremendously. Thank you for being my sisters and friends for so many years!!!

I hope you feel loved and celebrated through this small token of Thanksgiving. I would not have made it out of many of my "situations" if I didn't have your prayers and sweet words of encouragement. If the Lord blesses me with a fine chocolate man, you better believe I will have every last one of you by my side! You are my gift and treasure on this side of heaven, and I love you as much as I love "mint chocolate chip ice cream." Thank you for rooting me on over the years, fighting with and for me, and telling me the truth even when it hurts. Your friendship means the world to me, and I pray that the Lord blesses us with many more years to come. Kellee, I love you so much, and this love is for life! Ava, you are my favorite light skinned sister! Kasey, you are my little bestie! Heather, you are the realest! I love all of you!

STUDY QUESTIONS FOR BELIEVERS, TEACHERS, AND STUDENTS

Please answer these questions honestly and ask the Lord to meet you right where you are. The scriptures are a guide and reference for you as you journey on to freedom in Christ.

Believers:

How does your upbringing or past still affect you in the present?

How have your parents, other family members, or friends wounded you?

How do you think God views this tragedy or offense? How

would he want you to respond or deal with the pain of it? (Romans 8; Genesis 50; John 16; Psalm 147:3)

What does God do for those who mourn or deal with pain? (Psalm 147:3; Matthew 5:4; Psalm 34:18; Isaiah 53:4-6)

Are you carrying any undealt with unforgiveness? What does the bible say about
forgiveness? (Mark 11:25; Matthew 6:14-15; Ephesians 4: 26-27; Ephesians 4:32)

Are there any idols in your life that you need to confess to God? What does God say about confession? (Exodus 20:3-5; James 5:16; 1 John 1:9; Proverbs 28:13; Psalm 32:5)

TEACHERS

What is the why behind your job? In other words, why do you teach?

Are you glorifying God in every aspect of your teaching? How so? What does God say about work? (Colossians 3:23; Psalm 90:17; Proverbs 12:11; Proverbs 13:4)

Do you pray for your students, their parents, your coworkers, and your own mental stability? What does God say about prayer? (1 John 5:14-15; 1 Chronicles 16:8-12; 2 Chronicles 7:14; Ephesians 6:18)

Has teaching become your idol or god? Are you setting realistic boundaries with work? (Exodus 20:3-12)

How do you view "your job?" Are you still fulfilling the

"Great Commission?" What is the "Great Commission?" (Matthew 28:16-20)

How are you loving on your students? How are you building them up with your words rather than tearing them down? (Ephesians 4:29-32)

When you fall or mess up, are you quick to ask for forgiveness, confess your sins, and share your struggle with others? Why or why not?

What does God's grace look like for you at your job? What is grace? (2 Corinthians 12:8-9; Romans 3:20-24; John 1:14)

STUDENTS

How are you honoring God with your school work? What does it mean to honor God with your school work? (1 Corinthians 10:31; 1 Corinthians 6:20; Proverbs 3:9)

Who are your friends? Are your friends a good influence or bad influence on you? What does God say about the company you keep? (1 Corinthians 15:33; 2 Corinthians 6:14; Proverbs 13:20; Proverbs 14:7)

How are you respecting your teachers and other school authorities? What does the bible say about respect? Why should we respect those in authority? (Romans 13:1-7; Matthew 7:12; Romans 12; Philippians 2)

How are you honoring and obeying your parents' authority? What does the bible say about obeying your parents? (Ephesians 6:1-9)

STUDY QUESTIONS AND SCRIPTURES FOR PERSONAL GROWTH

Marriage, Singleness, Sex, Suicide, Community, and Freedom.

What does God say about singleness? What does God say about marriage? How should we view each season of life? (1 Corinthians 7:1-40; Genesis 2:18; Genesis 2:22-24; Proverbs 12:4; Proverbs 18:22; Ephesians 5:22-33)

How do you view your singleness? Is it a gift or a curse? Where did this thinking come from? How have you surrendered your viewpoint to the Lord?

How do you view your marriage or future marriage? What does it look like to honor God as a wife based on the scriptures above?

What does the bible say about sex? As a single woman, how

are you fleeing from sexual immorality? (Ephesians 5:33; Genesis 2:24; Hebrews 13:4; 1 Corinthians 6:12-20)

What does the bible say about sex for the married person? Are there any restrictions with sex in marriage? (1 Corinthians 6:12-10; 1 Corinthians 7; Matthew 5:28; 1 Thessalonians 4:3-5)

Does the bible speak to suicide? If you are struggling emotionally, how does God speak to your situation? Is there hope for the weary and heavy laden according to the bible? (Matthew 11:28-30; Psalm 34; Psalm 23)

Is community important to God? Is community important to you? What does God say about the body of Christ and the fellowship of the saints? (1 Corinthians 12:12-31; Romans 12:4-5; Ephesians 4:4; Hebrews 10:25)

What does the bible say about freedom? What does freedom look like for the believer? (Galatians 5:1; Galatians 5:13; 2 Corinthians 3:17; 1 Peter 2:16)

[1]How did I grow at CGM, and what did I do?

[2]How did CGM make me better? How did God change me? How did the Lord show me himself through others?

Black men/ the ways of Children pointed me to my relationship with the Lord.

Made in the USA
Lexington, KY
21 December 2019